the real work of leaders

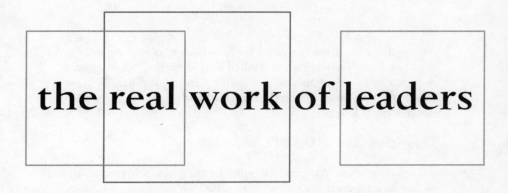

the real work of leaders

A REPORT FROM THE FRONT LINES OF MANAGEMENT

Donald L. Laurie

PERSEUS PUBLISHING
Cambridge, Massachusetts

Many of the designations used by manufacturers and sellers to distinguish their products are claimed as trademarks. Where those designations appear in this book and Perseus Publishing was aware of a trademark claim, the designations have been printed in initial capital letters.

Copyright © 2000 by Donald L. Laurie

Library of Congress Catalog Card Number: 00-102286
ISBN 0-7382-0249-5

Perseus Publishing is a member of the Perseus Books Group.

Find us on the World Wide Web at http://www.perseuspublishing.com

Perseus Publishing books are available at special discounts for bulk purchases in the U.S. by corporations, institutions, and other organizations. For more information, please contact the Special Markets Department at HarperCollins Publishers, 10 East 53rd Street, New York, NY 10022, or call 1-212-207-7528.

Text design by Jeff Williams
Set in 12-point Fairfield LH Light by Perseus Publishing Services

First printing, May 2000
1 2 3 4 5 6 7 8 9 10—03 02 01 00

To my beautiful ladies and the new sailor,
who have brought such joy to my life:
Susie, Meghan, Rhodie, Chantal, Madeleine, Isabella,
and Harrison Donald

Contents

Preface

Deep in the mountain forests of Rwanda, a band of gorillas awaken. They stretch and scratch, rummage and root in the thick foliage for something to eat. A pair of young males hoot and grunt in boisterous play as disinterested females look on. Suddenly, the dominant silverback, the group's leader, begins to move. Seeking direction, all the others turn to him, awaiting his lead to the watering hole and to new sources of food. He stretches his massive body, looks around, selects the path, and begins to lumber down the trail, with the rest of the band following in accepted order.

Along the way, the great silverback may pause to break up a fight between two young males attempting to assert territorial rights. Or he may assemble his band in a defensive stance when he catches the scent of an intruder, perhaps a wandering young lothario intent on snatching away females to establish his own family group. Whatever problems the band encounters, it looks to the old silverback for guidance. He manages internal disputes, controls behavior, establishes authority. And his leadership works, so long as the threat is from another gorilla or some other animal common to the Rwandan forest. Weighing 400 pounds and with an arm span approaching seven feet, the silverback has no peers in his own milieu. But if the group encounters a poacher with a stun gun who is attempting to capture a young gorilla for exhibit in a foreign zoo, the leader's physical strength and reach are of no consequence. The old silverback doesn't know how to respond to the new challenge.

Today, the business forest is teeming with new challengers packing stun guns. Globalization, cutthroat competition fueled by technological change, increasingly demanding consumers, and new opportunities and threats spawned by the Internet are only a few of the new realities that have profoundly altered the face of competition in confusing ways. Seldom have leaders at all levels confronted a more precarious business environment. And it has put them at risk. But not all the dangers come from outside. Lester Alberthal, former chairman and chief executive officer of Electronic Data Systems Corporation (EDS), based in Plano, Texas, has no doubt why almost all successful large companies eventually lose their edge. Listen to what Alberthal told me: "When you're extraordinarily successful, when you can do no wrong, when you are dominating a marketplace, and you've built something that's really fantastic and the world says, 'Isn't this wonderful?' the natural human tendency is to start institutionalizing it."

Everything becomes inwardly focused: the process of research, development, and designing, your process of thinking about the market, your education process. You say this is "the GM way," "this is our way." Although some of that speaks to your core competencies, once you become totally preoccupied with it, you ignore the marketplace. You wind up with a Cadillac, an Oldsmobile, or a Buick all looking exactly the same because the engineers have said this is the way to do it. But the marketplace says "we don't want that."

Or you do what IBM did—it ignored the personal computer and the demand of the marketplace for personalized technology and got a few years behind the curve. Once you do that, it becomes very difficult in a high-paced research and development

(R&D) environment to catch up. This is true regardless of how talented people are.

Alberthal's culprit is complacency, plain and simple. As old as human nature, and just as deadly, it is merely another of the factors—albeit of a company's own doing—that undermines corporate management structures and leads to their early demise.

Leadership has joined the ranks of dangerous professions. Chief executives, declares *Business Week,* "leave their jobs these days with the regularity of NFL coaches." Evidence backs them up. Studies show that corporate boards are three times more likely to oust a chief executive today than they were twenty years ago. Between August 1999 and January 2000, some sixty-six computer-industry executives vacated their posts; in the financial-services industry, some fifty-two executives departed. Those who do manage to remain often find themselves swept away in a takeover; witness Robert B. Palmer of Digital Equipment Corporation, Wolfgang A. Schmitt of Rubbermaid, Inc., and Thomas T. Stallkamp of Chrysler Corporation. Is it any wonder that many leaders feel as if they have lost their way? Much of what they knew and took for granted about managing their companies has been called into question.

I know firsthand about the problems leaders are encountering today and the wreckage strewn around corporate boardrooms here and abroad. For some twenty years now, I have advised the chief executive officers of *Fortune* 100 companies. It is from my observations of the environments in which these leaders are operating that this book was born. Three years in the making and featuring more than forty in-depth CEO interviews, it is designed to help current and future leaders and their organizations cope with the harsh, sometimes disorienting realities of today's business world.

I intend to simplify the act of leadership by providing a new and practical framework for understanding and practicing it. It is my hope that this book will enable leaders to ask tough questions that uncover the problems that can threaten the very existence of an organization. Leaders who orient their employees toward solving problems will find them more able to ward off the corroding dangers of complacency. The time is now for understanding the complex work that leaders do. Let's get on with *The Real Work of Leaders*.

Acknowledgments

I have learned the most from my work with clients. I have learned that real leadership can be performed by a CEO, a technologist with passion, a marketing person with insight, or an executive assistant with great administrative skills. I have seen real leadership in action at British Airways, IBM, Hewlett-Packard, Nokia, Warner Lambert, Johnson & Johnson, KPMG, Up To Date, Optigrab, and elsewhere.

The CEOs who participated in my research during the past four years have been generous with their time, experience, and insight. My special thanks to those who encouraged me to return to their offices for deeper discussion. Ralph Larsen of Johnson & Johnson, Gene Fife of Goldman Sachs, Roger Ackerman of Corning, Bernard Fournier of Rank Xerox, Colin Marshall of British Airways, Lew Platt of Hewlett-Packard, Ruud Koedijk of KPMG Netherlands, Doug Brown of Advent International, Paul Garwood of Unilever, and others.

There is a special group of intellectual and operational partners whose collaboration has enriched this work in thought and deed. Ron Heifetz of the Kennedy School of Government at Harvard University was my coauthor on the *Harvard Business Review* article, "Work of Leadership." That article was the genesis of this book. He has been an invaluable and generous resource. We have often written together and collaborated in the sometimes difficult task of working with the top teams of global corporations as they tackle the real work of leaders. Terri Munroe of San Diego University brought her unique insights to these challenges. Yves Doz, C.K. Prahalad, Gary Hamel, Michael Pieschewski, Susie Friedman, Suzanne Boulos, and Mike Placko have always been readily available as colleagues and friends.

Donna Carpenter of Wordworks was a wonderful collaborator. I have valued her professionalism and friendship. Along with Maurice Coyle, Ruth Hlavacek, Deborah Horvitz, and Robert W. Stock, Carpenter helped me shape my concepts and experiences into *The Real Work of Leaders*. Jill Adkins, Susan Higgins, Barbara Nelson, Toni Porcelli, Cindy Sammons, and John Sammons provided all of us with great research and administrative support throughout the project. Helen Rees, my literary agent, provided sage and pragmatic advice at critical points in the process. Nick Philipson of Perseus added great value in suggesting formidable editorial enhancements. Caro Fry, my assistant for the past ten years, has been an example of how to turn around production of impossible deadlines with a sense of good cheer. Candy McGann has been amazingly helpful in everything administrative during the past fifteen years.

I owe the most to my elegant wife, Susie. She is the source of the intangibles—a lifetime commitment together, loving support in the face of adversity, and a contagious confidence that this would all work out.

Don Laurie
Oyster Harbors
Osterville, Massachusetts
February 7, 2000

the real work of leaders

PART ONE

A Leader's Real Time

1

What Should Leaders Do?

ASK LEADERS WHAT THEIR REAL WORK IS, as I often do in my role as an adviser to senior managers, and you will get a variety of thoughtful answers. Then I pose another question: "If I had followed you around for the last four to six weeks, what would I conclude about your real work? In other words, what are your real priorities? How do you and other key executives in your organization spend your time day to day? Are your priorities linked to your work as a leader, as you have described it?" As you might expect, the answers vary. Many senior managers insist that their schedules support their image of themselves as leaders. Then, I ask to see their calendars—a revealing exercise. Often, they have spent little or no time in the past month on what they say matters most, not because they didn't want to. People do not overbook themselves on purpose, but crises often rule their calendars. Emergencies, by definition, arrive unannounced.

Ralph S. Larsen, chairman and chief executive officer of Johnson & Johnson (J&J), the largest health-care products company in the world, told me a story about a reporter for a New York City television station implicating a J&J product in the death of a patient. "I *have* to step away and deal with that kind of emergency," Larsen told me.

Invariably, when leaders confront the truth about how they spend their time, they tell me the last month was "unusual." One of my favorite comments came from Jan Carlzon, who was then chief executive officer of Scandinavian Airlines System (SAS), the $5.2-billion-a-year passenger and cargo carrier based in Stockholm, Sweden. After Carlzon defined his work as setting strategy, I asked him how much time he had spent on it during the past month. He thought for a minute, and then said with a smile: "Oh, you'd conclude I was a liar. I'm not the leader I just described." Truth is, most leaders are not the leaders they describe. That is, they aren't engaged in the real work of leadership. Being a leader is not easy and never has been. But today more than ever, leaders confront a complex list of problems as they attempt to guide their organizations toward growth and prosperity.

This book describes how you, as a leader, can and must nurture your awareness of problems, recognize them, and fortify your organization to meet and solve them. In business, the primary mission of the manager as leader is to mobilize people— your superiors, subordinates, lateral colleagues, and outside parties—to engage in their work. And this requires everyone to define, refine, and resolve problems. Solving problems—or, more accurately, enabling *others* to solve problems—is the leaders' real work. By identifying and framing problems, a leader jump-starts the crucial process of marshaling the resources needed to eliminate them.

Am I being too negative with my emphasis on problem solving? I think not. Confronting problems will lead to their resolution; avoiding them is not only "negative," it is dangerous. I have on my desk a brass paperweight in the shape of a Chinese character that stands for "problem." But it has a second meaning: "opportunity." In other words, every business problem and every

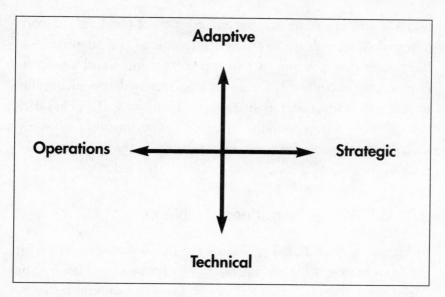

The problem(s) we are trying to solve.

business risk contains the seeds of business opportunity. The Internet serves as a useful example. At one level, it allows new competitors to assault and sabotage a company while simultaneously it opens a strategic window of opportunity to create new relationships with customers and suppliers, reduce selling and distribution costs, and even invent new businesses.

In this book, I provide leaders with an approach that can simplify and speed up the task of addressing business problems, as well as help them prepare their organizations to harvest their inherent and unique opportunities. My leadership framework (above) encompasses both problems and the work necessary to arrive at effective solutions. It reflects the experience I have gained advising dozens of organizations in the United States and Europe, as well as the wisdom of the many successful leaders I have interviewed along the way.

The top half of the framework enables you to place your problems (a.k.a. opportunities) into one of two categories: operational or strategic. The bottom half consists of two kinds of work required to address these problems: technical and adaptive. Solutions, however, come in two forms: technical and adaptive. Highly categorized, this framework is designed specifically for businesses and other organizations. Leaders will necessarily have to tailor solutions to their particular circumstances, but my four-part outline can serve as a framework for that process. Let's start by looking at the kinds of problems that exist.

Operational Problems

In business, operational problems are those that interfere with the systems we have set up for the purpose of achieving our goals. They also challenge leaders' abilities to maintain a steady, incremental improvement in performance.

Centuries ago, herds of musk oxen roamed the Alaskan tundra. They were hunted by packs of hungry wolves who tried to separate calves and sickly oxen from the rest of the herd. The musk oxen responded with an effective, protective defense: The herd formed a tight group and stood fast, horns out, in the direction of the threat. The result? Whenever wolves approached the herd, the musk oxen practiced a response they had learned over time, and the wolves were kept at bay. Although the details may change (the number of preying wolves or the time of an attack, for example), the outcome is still dependent on the special adjustments that the oxen made to any given assault—that is, how well they were able to execute their basic strategy. For the oxen, wolves were an operational problem.

Why did the Eastman Kodak Company force out its chairman and chief executive officer, Kay Whitmore? At the time, most analysts blamed his inability to find the right strategy to make the company a major force in digital photography. In fact, Kodak had already adopted a plan to move into digital imaging before

Whitmore took over. Whitmore's problem was operational. He did not put the correct systems into place and he failed to inspire workers to respond in such a way that would have enabled Kodak to execute its new digital strategy. And neither did his successor, George M. C. Fisher.

After assuming the post of chairman and chief executive officer in 1993, Fisher neither succeeded in reviving Kodak's business nor realized the company's goal of becoming a major player in digital imaging. In reports published the day he announced he was stepping down as chief executive, Fisher said he felt the time was right for a change in leadership. Analysts said that the executive had waited too long to cut costs, but I say he failed to solve a key internal operational problem.

Strategic Problems

In business, a strategic problem may appear in the form of discontinuity—changes like globalization, to say nothing of the Internet—that rewrite the rules and make accepted methods of competing as obsolete as Sanskrit.

The Alaskan musk ox was quite capable of dealing with its operational problem—that is, hungry wolves. But when human hunters arrived, armed first with spears and later rifles, the tight-group defense was no longer effective. In fact, it played into the hunters' hands, turning the entire herd into a single, vulnerable target for their spears and guns. Clearly, the oxen were now confronted with a different kind of problem that could be solved neither by making small adjustments in the existing strategy nor by changing the way in which the strategy was carried out. The strategy itself needed to be changed, and changed dramatically. The musk oxen faced a strategic problem. Because they were unable to address it, they were wiped out by hunters. Their population didn't reappear until the 1930s, with imports from Greenland. Decades later, the herds were so well rejuvenated that when China's Communist Party leader Mao Zedong made a goodwill gesture to the United States by sending a pair of giant pandas, the United States could afford to reciprocate by shipping back a pair of musk oxen.

Discontinuities can make or break companies and even whole industries. The record business, a current case in point, was shaken to its core when the cassette made the old vinyl LPs extinct, only for cassettes to be challenged by CDs. Now, the threat is MP3, a technology that allows consumers to download recorded music from the Internet.

Discontinuities, says Michael Fradette, a partner in Deloitte & Touche Consulting, in Boston, Massachusetts, make a mockery of the very notion of long-range planning. Every sign indicates that they are going to continue and even multiply. "We must," he urges, "find new ways to think about these discontinuities, to organize our enterprises to exploit them, and to turn them to extraordinary advantage." Strategic problems also occur when a competitor creates a discontinuity that affects distribution, manufacturing, customer relations, or technology.

Similarly, in the 1980s, International Business Machines Corporation (IBM), the pride of corporate America, faced a strategic problem par excellence. Dell Computer Corporation introduced direct sales and customer-ordered assembly and assembly units with standard parts as though they were Lego pieces. This enabled Dell to sell PCs at prices as much as 40 percent below those of IBM. Other competitors, like Compaq Computer Corporation, replicated Dell's innovative approach. As a consequence, IBM's share of the personal-computer market plunged from 45.9 percent to 14.2 percent almost overnight. No matter what efficiencies it might introduce, Big Blue's network of sellers, resellers, and retailers could never compete on price with its new competitors. It needed to rethink the way it marketed its products or get out of the business.

Around the same time, because senior managers at television networks ABC, NBC, and CBS failed to respond to a demographic revolution in the making, they found themselves confronting a strategic problem called Cable News Network (CNN). It happened because Robert E. (Ted) Turner III recognized the revolution while the major networks were preoccupied with a minor skirmish. I hasten to add that, in both cases—the television networks and IBM—executives were not left out in the cold because they were too stupid to understand what was happening.

Spending so much time fighting to put out brushfires encountered in the normal course of business means that little time is spent deciphering structural changes in a particular industry or thinking through the implications of those changes for the future of the company. By the time executives realize the gravity of a situation, it is often too late to head off very serious complications. So whereas the networks agonized over the public's willingness to watch an hour-long news program during the dinner hour, Turner exploited a series of demographic shifts. One was the fact that the number of families with two working parents had risen dramatically since the 1960s. Nearly 55 percent of American women were in the job market, twice the percentage of the 1940s, and many of them had work schedules different from their husbands. It was farewell to the family reunion around the television set every evening at six o'clock. Meanwhile, the number of older retirees had doubled between 1950 and 1980.

Turner realized that these changes were vastly increasing the potential daytime and late-hour television audience. He thought he could capture a sizable chunk of that audience by offering news around the clock. Now the networks are playing catch-up, inventing their own versions of his Atlanta, Georgia–based CNN. They face an uphill struggle, however. Having failed to respond to the demographic changes, the strategic problem, they missed the opportunity to seize the advantage.

Categorizing problems as either operational or strategic, then, is the first stage in the process in which business leaders solve such problems. The second stage calls for them to categorize the work that needs to be done as adaptive or technical, or sometimes a combination of the two, which will then allow leaders to uncover the best solution to a problem.

One of the framework's key advantages is that it simplifies a leader's world. It cuts through the forest of management rhetoric and transformation theories. It shows that the real work of the leader can be understood and organized within the narrow compass of two kinds of problems, operational and strategic, if the technical and/or adaptive components of possible solutions are applied.

Technical Work

Technical work is routine work. Changes are those made by adjusting current operations. Technical work is the appropriate choice when what needs to be done is apparent, the resources for performing the changes are available, and the capability to make the needed change is also available. Execution is key. The technical components of a solution may include investing in the latest model of a machine tool to speed up lagging production time or building a new factory to boost production capacity. Calling for reports and meetings to discuss and decide the company's response to a competitor's new product is another example. Sound boring? It is actually the real work of leaders.

John F. Welch Jr., the legendary chairman and chief executive officer of the General Electric Company, Fairfield, Connecticut, maintains a steady focus on whatever problem is most immediate. At meetings, he takes notes on what decisions have been made and who is responsible for implementing each aspect. And he follows up. He makes it abundantly clear that he expects people to meet their commitments.

Lawrence A. Bossidy, chairman of Honeywell, Inc., since it merged with his AlliedSignal, Inc., the $15-billion-a-year manufacturer of aerospace equipment, auto parts, and other products based in Morristown, New Jersey, believes that if you are "armed with a clear picture of where you are, a clear vision of where you want to go, and a clear plan of how to get there, the only question that remains is: Can you execute? That is what differentiates one leader from another."

When Eckhard Pfeiffer was ousted as chief executive officer of Houston, Texas-based Compaq Computer, analysts blamed his failure to come up with a grand new strategy. But Benjamin Rosen, Compaq's chairman, had a different explanation. The strategy was fine, he said, at the time, but Pfeiffer's execution was weak. "Our plans," Rosen told a reporter, "are to speed up decision making and make the company more efficient." In other words, what Rosen was looking for in a leader was someone who could handle what is essentially the bread and butter of leadership: successful execution. Companies rarely fail or die because they don't have a strategy. They die because they don't forcefully execute that strategy. James O'Connor of Ford Motor Company once told me that "execution is about helping people to learn what they must do differently to adapt to change."

In company after company, I have seen enormous talent and energy applied to developing the right strategy, only to have the players drop the ball when it came to implementation. If the right answer is not implemented effectively, it may just as well have remained undiscovered. Compaq's Rosen wanted someone who could figure out the technical work required to address a given problem or problems; he wanted someone who could find the right people for each task, make sure they delivered on their commitments, and keep improving the company's performance.

Although technical work is a part of many solutions, most examples of using technical work alone date back to the 1960s, 1970s, and early 1980s. During that time, senior executives primarily called on their experience and expertise to cope with problems related to plans, budgets, control systems, and other technical aspects of the business. Such problems required adjustment, but little adaptation, by individuals or groups within the organization.

Here is an example of the technical-only approach: A company leader decides to shift some of the company's manufacturing to a low-cost area, say from South Carolina to South Korea. The leader, who has already closed three or four other U.S. factories and knows how to release employees efficiently and humanely, has experience with other Far East manufacturers. In this case, he or she knows better than his or her staff how the job should be done, and can thus provide the technical solution.

Adaptive Work

Although solutions for dealing with operational problems quite frequently require adaptive work, solutions to strategic problems always do. That spells trouble, because adaptive work demands more of the entire workforce, leader included, than technical work. Adaptive work lies at the core of a company's ability to succeed. Because it often requires new ideas and attitudes that compete with established values, however, it calls for learning the new and unlearning the old. And that can be a tumultuous process. Because it is the most complex and difficult of the four elements of my leadership framework, adaptive work demands the lion's share of attention in this book. In fact, it is the focus of part two. Some idea of what is involved can be gleaned from a glimpse at Haworth, Inc., a leading office-furniture manufacturer, based in Holland, Michigan.

When Haworth's leaders recognized that their company needed a major revitalization, they decided to transform it into a just-in-time organization, producing made-to-order office products with no inventory. They knew, however, to achieve that goal would require a metamorphosis in the viewpoint and values of every employee from top to bottom because the adaptive change was challenging deeply-held beliefs and the management habits of a lifetime. A series of study groups was set up and all employees were enrolled. They were instructed in the fundamentals of the just-in-time system, which included an emphasis on constantly improving performance. Gradually, and with considerable difficulty, workers mastered new skills and attitudes and the transformation was accomplished. Moreover, the emphasis on education and keeping workers informed has become a fixed part of the Haworth culture. The study groups now cover not only the just-in-time issues, but also current strategic issues facing the company. To develop and implement solutions for their company's problems, leaders must define the issues and take action that will help people in their organizations engage in technical and adaptive work, or a combination of the two.

Perhaps the physician's role can be used as an analogy. Patients and their families consult physicians for solutions, and physicians attempt to provide what their patients want—a diagnosis and treatment that will lead to a cure, which is, of course, the ultimate solution. Such an arrangement works fine in some situations. To a patient with an infection, for example, the physician can often offer the perfect solution: "Here's a tetracy-cline prescription. Take it four times a day. Call me if there's a problem." The patient gets better, experiences no side effects from the medicine, pays a minimal fee, and feels extremely grateful to the doctor. The physician has engaged in technical work. The problem was defined, treated, and cured by the doc-tor exercising his or her expertise. Aside from taking pills as pre-scribed and accurately describing his or her symptoms, nothing was expected of the patient. The whole weight of identifying the problem and solving it fell on the doctor.

More common, however, are situations that require work by both the doctor and the patient. The doctor can define the prob-lem and even undertake some remedies—some technical work—but cannot provide a complete cure. For that to happen, the patient must do some adaptive work. For example, a patient suffering from heart disease may be restored to health. The physician makes the diagnosis, prescribes medications, even performs triple bypass surgery, which is technical work for the doctor. Ultimately, however, the patient's health is likely to de-pend on his or her willingness to make lifestyle changes, which may mean changing diet, giving up smoking, increasing exercise and walking, and perhaps even leaving a too-stressful job. For many patients, the choice is to adapt or die.

Yet sometimes no amount of technical and adaptive work on the doctor's part will result in a cure. The solution to the prob-lem depends in large part, if not totally, on the patient's willing-ness to assume responsibility for making lifestyle changes. Examples of illnesses in this category include, but are not re-stricted to, alcoholism and certain eating disorders, such as anorexia and bulimia. In these cases, the physician's scalpel and prescription pad are of little use. The doctor can diagnose the problem and explain it to the patient, but he or she must do the adaptive work necessary to recovery.

A better description of the physician's job in such a case might be helping the patient to do the work only he or she can do. Like the physician, the business leader confronts many problems that call for adaptive work on the part of employees. These problems are messy. Inevitably, large numbers of people are involved, many of whom will disagree with how the problem is defined, as well as how to treat it. Topside executives and middle managers throughout the organization will bring different experiences and perceptions to the table. Different outcomes will affect their responsibilities and careers in distinct ways. Given the massive structural changes within industries, the emergence of global competitors, rapid technological innovation, and the persistence of obsolete organizational structures and management systems, just defining problems is a challenge today. Add the changes in customer expectations and you have few problems that will yield to technical expertise alone—and many that require adaptive work. No one leader can handle all that, particularly when an organization must undergo the wrenching readjustment of attitudes and actions. The heavy lifting must be taken on by those most directly affected and involved. Think of it in terms of war. For a nation to successfully fight a war, the mass of its citizens must be willing to change their lives if necessary—to adapt.

In Winston Churchill's first major statement as Britain's prime minister during World War II, he declared: "I have nothing to offer but blood, toil, tears, and sweat." He was defining the work and sacrifices his nation and its people would have to make. Essentially, he was framing the problem for the people of Britain: Would his listeners have the courage and the will to do the job? Would they take responsibility for the work only they could do? Leaders of successful business transformations at companies like General Electric, Ford Motor Company, British Airways Plc, and British information technology provider ICL Plc have taken an approach similar to Churchill's. Instead of answers, they offer questions. And from the answers they create a vision, what I call an ambition, that will propel their troops to greater heights. Ambition is what you want to be. Strategy is how you go about realizing it. Leaders set the ambition.

Setting ambition is the first step on the road to solving the most difficult kinds of business problems—those that require fundamental changes in the ways people work. Technical solutions provided by command-and-control executives are inadequate in these situations. Edicts from on high cannot achieve the increased speed, flexibility, mutual support, and trust across functions that are needed to gain greater customer responsiveness. This solution must be discovered by individuals and groups throughout the organization.

When Sir Colin Marshall took the helm at British Airways (BA), he determined that the only way the airline could become responsive to its customers was to alter the way his workers related to the customer and to each other. Functional "silos" had to be destroyed, people had to be able to use their authority in their own area of responsibility, and trust among the workers needed to be restored. During the three years I worked with BA, Sir Colin continually represented the customer and frontline workers in every problem-solving discussion. He engaged the top 1,000 managers in learning initiatives that enabled them to understand his ambition—and the adaptive role of each department and individual in achieving it. But Sir Colin's decision to hand over responsibility to those on the front lines was not without its pitfalls. People do not always use their responsibility wisely. In one instance, when a soccer player missed a London flight his team had chartered to take them to a match in Scotland, a BA employee used his newfound authority to charter a separate flight for the latecomer. Needless to say, Sir Colin had to rein in such reckless behavior.

What happens when leaders ignore adaptive work? When George Bush was elected president of the United States, he quickly sought to make good on his campaign promise to "win the war on drugs." He began by appointing a "drug czar," increasing the Coast Guard's budget for surveillance, declaring war on the Colombia drug barons, and arresting General Manuel Noriega of Panama for his role as an intermediary. The result? After four years, the drug problem had only worsened. George Bush's technical solution, which had seemed like an obvious, logical answer, failed. The reason? The president and his advisers didn't engage schools, parents, and communities in the war on drugs. In other words, they ignored the locus of responsibility, and neglected to tackle the problem where it existed.

You can't solve that kind of a complex, strategic problem without the wholehearted support of the country's families and communities. The expertise of the president and his surrogates could not substitute for the adaptive changes required from the public. If churches, schools, and the family unit could not or would not adapt, the problem was not going to be solved.

On the other end of the solution continuum, my friend and colleague Ronald A. Heifetz, director of the Leadership Education Project at the Kennedy School of Government at Harvard University, likes to tell a story concerning a chemical plant that was thought to be responsible for an unusually high incidence of leukemia in the community in which it was located. Because the plant was the community's main employer and its payroll was critical to the town's survival, townspeople and company representatives worked together to find a technical and adaptive solution that both sides could support. The result? The problem was corrected, and the plant survived.

What Should One Do?

I encourage the executives with whom I work to make a list of the major operational and strategic problems facing businesses and their leaders today. They list these problems on one side of a sheet of paper or white board. Then I ask them to set up two columns, one labeled "technical" and one labeled "adaptive." I ask them to determine the heading their problems fall under. Almost always, many of the problems are adaptive, especially when they have crossfunctional or crossbusiness implications.

What often heads the list? That value today is determined by *customers,* not products and services, reflects a change to which businesses must adjust. In the first hundred years of the industrial age, a business leader's aim was to exploit the first stage of what we now call the *value chain.* The links of this chain included raw materials, patents on innovations, and the skills and knowledge acquired by education and hard work. Therein lay the starting point of many early companies. Businesses were built and fortunes were made, largely out of coal, oil, iron, textiles, and railroads. As the industrial revolution gathered force, business leaders began to exploit production capabilities. Consider a staple product such as milk. Farmers used to produce milk that was delivered in bottles directly to neighborhood customers. Distribution became more sophisticated, production capabilities were developed, and dairies emerged. People no longer bought directly from the farmer, but rather from dairies and their distribution channels.

The next stage saw larger, value-added players who greatly expanded product and service. Whereas once dairy products basically meant milk and cream, today consumers can choose milk with various fat, vitamin, and calcium contents, not to mention an assortment of yogurts, cheeses, and butters offering the same nutritional options. The dairy aisle in the supermarket is over-flowing with choice. Producers have come to recognize that a product can be sold in a number of different ways. If they can't exploit the raw material or production capabilities, they must turn their attention to other methods of persuasion.

Another everyday household product, salt, offers a case in point. Its price can range from pennies to dollars a pound. But salt is salt. Apart from variations in coarseness, the difference is not so much in the product itself as in the packaging, branding, and advertising. The focus has switched to the relationship with customers who have chosen to buy a particular brand of salt. The customer base, rather than the product, has become the real driver of value.

"Find a niche" used to be the standard advice to businesspeople, just as "specialization" still is in medicine. Today, however, when everyone is trying to elbow into specialized niches, success lies in exploiting the relationship with the customer. Business leaders can no longer rely on a product to sell itself; customers must be wooed. So the complexity of the customer "problem" only increases. Still, if customers are properly taken care of, profitability lies within any leader's grasp. Thus the make-or-break question becomes: Who manages this prime asset? The answer is, the front line.

Take a look at the other items on my list of problems. See how many apply to you.

- Markets have evolved from local to regional to global. Once, during a business lunch, an executive demonstrated globalization by ordering what I jokingly referred to as a "global salad," because it included lettuce from Argentina, tomatoes from Italy, avocados from California, water chestnuts from China, and spring onions from Spain.

- Billion-dollar divisions of the same company are locked in margin battles in ruthlessly competitive industries. Some such divisions have started questioning the value of being part of a corporation.
- Disruptive technologies create the conditions within which new business models that destroy yesterday's notions about competition can be invented.
- Customers are better educated about their product alternatives and more insistent on getting just what they want.
- The demand for well-trained workers has soared, accelerated by the fact that the best people are more knowledgeable about their increased options as well as about their own value on the market.
- Knowledge and competencies are harder to share within a corporation if it enters the global market, as so many do today. Even blood ties weaken with distance, and as military history teaches us, long lines of communication can spell defeat.
- Large companies lose the entrepreneurial impetus needed to invent and incubate new businesses.
- Wall Street analysts often seem to know more about the company than the company's own senior managers.

In the face of such daunting problems, leaders must define objectives, set strategy, allocate resources, and make sure the components mesh and meld effectively. Yet there exists a present—though not always clear—danger in defining the leader and his or her role. The danger lies in the tendency to confuse leadership with authority when, in fact, they perform two different functions within an organization.

Authority is associated with specific formal and informal titles or positions. The formal position of financial vice president, for example, is defined by the authority to oversee specific departmental activities, direct particular projects, and manage certain people's access to capital. People are given positions and the authority that goes with them to undertake some piece of work and solve the problems that accompany it. In clear-cut, run-of-the-mill situations, that approach often will be successful. For example, it may work when the knowledgeable production manager tells the machine-tool operators how to gear up for a new part. But in the increasingly frequent situations wherein the nature of the problem is unclear and the values or guiding principles of various constituents are different, leadership and authority must part company.

The real work of leadership is not easy, precisely because it is not clear-cut, like that of, say, a financial vice president. The position draws on every facet of the leader's "being"; at times, his or her personality will be just as important as a specific area of expertise. It is no surprise that people in authority often develop ingenious rationalizations and patterns of behavior to avoid leadership. Then, these patterns of avoidance are perceived as normal. When authority fails, however, we erroneously call it a "crisis of leadership," blaming those in authority for their fake remedies and diversions. But we are partly at fault, too. We may be impatiently demanding a "quick fix" that prompts those with authority (who want to maintain it) to make unrealistic promises. When the promises fall through, we scapegoat the leaders and look for someone with fresh promises. Therein lies the rub. If authorities provide the "quick fix" the public demands of them, they may be setting a course that will require emergency intervention, both for themselves and their employees. Maybe the gathering storm will hit on someone else's watch and they will escape unscathed; maybe not. We have seen many chief executives fall in recent years as problems festered into crises.

Today, what is required of leadership is that it transcend the expectations inherent in the leader's authority. The real work of the leader is not to provide pat solutions, but to mobilize the group to work on the problem. When Mohandas Gandhi decided to fast, he did so not to *solve* the problems of his day, but to *engage* people in those problems. Fasting was not a solution. Fasting was intended to provoke questions and involvement, to inspire people to take greater responsibility for their destiny. In other words, it was an act of leadership.

Next

I should give you fair warning that my ideas challenge some of the fundamental tenets of traditional management thinking. For example, I show how leaders can sabotage their own and their companies' futures by insisting on their right to solve all problems while ignoring the potentially more relevant and powerful solutions stored in the minds of their workforce.

Instead of smoothing over and burying conflicts, I recommend that leaders elicit discussion of disputes and help those in conflict work through their issues. Instead of focusing only on hard numbers and tangible data, leaders must also attend to values. The real work of leaders, then, is to create the conditions that enable the whole workforce to adapt to change and participate in solving the problems their organizations face. To that end, I have formulated seven essential acts of leadership.

The first act calls on leaders to get on the balcony, meaning that they should remove themselves for a time from day-to-day routine so that they can view their company's reality as a whole. The second act is to communicate that reality to everyone in the organization. The third essential act of leadership deals with clarifying competing values, such as individualism versus teamwork—neither of which is bad or good, but one or another may be ill suited to the task at hand. The fourth directs leaders to advocate changes in values, if that is indicated to achieve the leader's ambition. The fifth act is to promote dialogue and discussion rather than seek an undemanding, easy consensus. The sixth act calls on leaders to modulate distress rather than simply relieve it, and the seventh requires that individuals take responsibility for solving problems that only she or he can solve—in other words, problems relating to one's personal job performance.

All of the acts of leadership are discussed and illustrated with corporate case histories in the chapters ahead. But first, let's look at how leaders in some of the world's most respected organizations are meeting strategic problems head-on by applying technical and adaptive solutions. I think you will find their real-life experiences enlightening, both in terms of understanding my terminology and in seeing just how my concepts fit into today's business milieu.

2

How Should Leaders Do What They Do?

A FEW YEARS AGO, DONALD L. BOUDREAU, vice chairman of Chase Manhattan Corporation, was among a group of bank executives who were invited to meet with William H. Gates III, chairman and chief executive officer of Microsoft Corporation. In the course of a wide-ranging discussion, Gates took pains to inform his guests that Microsoft had no plan to compete with them. According to Boudreau, Gates said, "Don't worry. We don't want to be a bank." In his pointed response—Chase doesn't "want to be a bank either"—Boudreau previewed what was to become his company's central guiding principle. It is what I call, simply, *ambition:* what the company strives to be.

Chase, in Boudreau's words, intended to provide consumers with "comprehensive financial solutions, however, wherever, and whenever they want." Put another way, the company's ambition was to be all things financial to all people, and that was a tall order. It meant, for example, competing with giant companies from outside the banking industry—like Microsoft. But Chase was emphatically committed to the concept of full service, since a decade before, its leaders confronted a potentially devastating strategic problem, comprised of three linked phenomena: new competition, expanded customer expectations, and the power of information technology.

Before I discuss the specifics of Chase's predicament and, ultimately, its resolution, let me express their magnitude by saying that this problem—and any attempt to deal with it—was bound to transform just about every aspect of Chase's business. It is the specter of precisely such life-changing corporate dilemmas that haunts business leaders everywhere. As Morgan Morton, president of a division of the Warner-Lambert Company in Morris Plains, New Jersey, once told me: "What keeps me awake at night is wondering who is going to come along and reinvent my business." Surely, many a sleepless night can be blamed on the likes of Charles R. Schwab (who reinvented financial services with the company that bears his name), Stephen M. Case (who reinvented information services with America Online, Inc.), Jeffrey P. Bezos (who reinvented bookselling with Amazon.com, Inc.), and Thomas G. Stemberg (who reinvented office supplies with Staples, Inc.). These businesspeople envisioned a future quite different from the present; they discerned emerging customer needs within that future, and set about meeting them—much to the consternation of their more traditional competitors.

In our personal lives, we are all familiar with the potential power of a strategic problem. We sense that something really big, posing a major challenge to the way we have been living, is about to happen. And we are right. It may be an opportunity to leave our current employer and join a start-up company. It could be the first hint of a crucial downsizing, or it may even be our first encounter with the person we marry.

In the case of Chase Manhattan, the threefold strategic problem—competition, customers, and technology—inspired the company's leaders to embark on both technical and adaptive work to discover a solution. From a technical perspective, the company knew that upgrading its information technology was necessary. With competition sprouting in unexpected places and customers demanding ever more sophisticated products and services, nothing less than a state-of-the-art information-technology system would do. Thus, enhanced technological capability was placed at the service of every customer and employee.

In the past, Boudreau noted in a recent speech, the company's method for acquiring new customers and selling to existing ones was less than methodical—"almost like throwing millions of pieces of direct mail or in-branch brochures up against a wall and hoping that some of them stuck." The new information-technology system, however, stores and "remembers" every bit of data about each transaction a consumer has with the organization, making it possible to predict when or if that consumer is likely to buy a particular product or service. The technology also enables the bank to evaluate whether that consumer is likely to switch to a competitor and, if so, at what price point such a move might be prevented.

Significantly, such information and analysis is instantaneously available to sales representatives at their work stations. When a customer calls the bank, his or her entire financial history automatically appears on the salesperson's computer screen. The customer's preferences regarding products and services and how he or she usually accesses them, as well as his or her customer status at Chase, is immediately available to the sales representative, who then is able to make decisions on the spot with respect to loans, product upgrades, or offers from the competition.

Although the technical component of Chase's solution—its sophisticated information system—placed a wealth of customer data at employees' fingertips, realizing its full value required Chase representatives to learn how to talk to customers in a new way. This adaptive component entailed changing the organization's culture and basic attitude toward, and relationship with, its customers. Chase employees, including tellers, lending agents, and financial planners, had to unlearn old ways of dealing with customers and learn totally new ones. Transformations of this importance evoke tough questions for leaders who must assess the company's capabilities and resources: Can the employees change their work habits? Should some employees be let go? What do we all need to learn and unlearn, and how can I help effect these changes?

According to Boudreau, the new culture at Chase mandates that "technology is everybody's business. Some senior managers may still be somewhat mystified by talk about gigabytes and multiple parallel processors. But you can be sure the successful ones will understand—and will constantly be learning more about—what technology can deliver to their customers and to the bottom line of their business." One example of the new technology's major effects is reflected by the fact that Chase sales representatives no longer have to sit passively at their branch offices awaiting the arrival of customers in person to discuss their needs. The staff, having learned an entirely new way of assisting customers, is now armed with information predicting which products and services a specific consumer may find useful at any stage in her or his business and personal life. Thus assuming an active role and anticipating their clients' needs, the sales representatives initiate contact with them bearing individually tailored information, and do so via the method of contact the customer prefers

Today, most bank business is done at automated teller machines (ATMs), by phone, or on the Internet. Only 3 million of Chase's 25 million customers have any relationship with its branch banks. About 40 percent of its retail mortgage business originates on loan officers' laptop computers, used not in the Chase Manhattan employee's office but in customers' offices and homes. Chase's experience illustrates how the technical and adaptive components of a solution, state-of-the-art technology, and a new way of relating to customers work together to solve a strategic problem. The result is the successful realization of Chase's ambition: to be all things financial to all people.

The leaders' role at Chase was to conceptualize their problem in such a way that its solution lay in intervention framed by and based on the technical and adaptive strategies I have been discussing. Crucially, the leaders' role did *not* include involvement in the nitty-gritty details that too often waste a large percentage of a leader's work hours. Many leaders feel that they personally must tend to every aspect of the solution, losing sight of the fact that their primary job is to set the agenda, determine the goals, find those who can best achieve them, and then delegate responsibility to the right people within the organization.

Jan Carlzon once wrote: "A leader is not appointed because he knows everything and can make every decision. He is appointed to bring together the knowledge that is available and then create the prerequisites for the work to be done. He creates the systems that enable him to delegate responsibility for day-to-day operations." The real work of the leader, then, is to identify the problem, frame it, explain it to people who are able to conceive a solution, and then sell that solution to everyone in the organization.

As we shall see in the chapters ahead, leaders must help people understand their current challenge by contextualizing its circumstances within the company's history. In addition, they must represent the organization's options as fully as possible, even if, at the outset, they are unaware of every possibility.

The interaction of technical and adaptive components for the purpose of effecting a solution, as we saw at Chase Manhattan, is not unusual. It is typical for a leader to devise a technical initiative—building a new factory to gain production efficiency, for example—and then find that the new factory requires adaptive work, both in the way the company functions as well as in the corporate culture. In the following pages, you will see how the elements of the leadership framework are enacted, specifically in an example featuring Johnson & Johnson, the manufacturer of health care products with the most comprehensive and broad base in the world. The emphasis will be on the solution's adaptive component because this aspect is most likely to present the leader's greatest difficulties. It requires nothing less of people than to transform their behavior.

In view of the changes buffeting the economic landscape, including globalization, cross-boundary competition, and frequent, major company mergers, many business leaders have recently restructured their operations. They have divested, delayered, and downsized. They have reengineered processes through total quality management (TQM), time-based management initiatives, and a new focus on customer satisfaction.

Although some of these initiatives have produced short-term gains, few leaders have made the internal changes essential for coping with strategic and operational problems over the long term. Like the musk oxen who could not change their protective strategy when confronted by a new enemy, and thus failed to adapt, too many leaders are working within outdated cultures predicated on a system of values that does not reflect today's realities. I am using "culture," which I will refer to throughout this book, to mean a set of ideals, attitudes, values, and understanding shared by the company's employees. Although overlooked by many business leaders, the essential element in any successful organization is the capacity to take effective, collective action.

Teamwork is not just a slogan; it is a necessity. The culture determines whether the collective action of teamwork is possible or impossible.

When he talks to business groups, Benjamin Zander, conductor of the Boston Philharmonic Orchestra, often discusses the role of the leader. First, he points out that he is the only musician in the orchestra who is silent. His effectiveness is measured by the degree to which he can make other musicians, his players, powerful. Then he adds: "When I realized that [conducting] was not about overpowering or influencing my players but about releasing their capacity to play, it was a transformation. The conductor is a sometimes silent releaser of the players' energies."

In the business context, too, leaders of adaptive efforts must be facilitators. Business today, however, is more like a jazz combo than Zander's symphonic orchestra. Performers must constantly improvise. The best leaders sense that jamming frequently produces the hottest, most distinctive sounds. Nevertheless, individual commitment to the common goal is still required. To achieve that goal, leaders must challenge members of the organization to explore and, if necessary, change their values in areas that affect the capacity for collective action.

When I asked Lewis E. Platt, chairman of the Hewlett-Packard Company, to describe his role as a leader, he emphasized his highest priority as "creating a wonderful environment in which others will be successful at finding the right answers." Referring to his primary responsibilities as "multifold," he said they include "setting and preserving and moving forward an environment. . . . [At HP], it's management by cultural control. We're very Japanese in that respect." And that pervasive culture is determined by "a very strong set of values which have been around since the '50s. They've not only been around . . . they're written down, they're articulated, they're discussed, we live by them every day." Unlike the corporation's objectives that are modified as the company grows, its "timeless" values have not been altered in fifty years. Crucial to HP's success is the effort invested in creating "an environment where people understand those values, [and] try to live by them." Platt believes that if the leader "can set that context, really have it work for you, not just [words] . . . on a piece of paper, then you can have a pretty high energy company without a lot of rules and regulations and policy books." Another successful company whose management style and operating procedures are driven by the concept of culture, and its most important component—values, is Nordstrom, Inc.

Challenging the status quo, the adaptive components of solutions, by definition, require learning and unlearning and, as in any process of change, a certain level of discomfort cannot be avoided. Although an agreeable and like-minded organizational culture can be productive, leaders of adaptive initiatives are not solely concerned with achieving consensus. Their job, which is to frame the problem in its entirety, takes place within the context of a spirited discussion wherein each employee feels comfortable expressing her or his ideas and feelings, even if they are in conflict with someone else's. It is imperative for workers to trust each other in the sense that they can rely on each other when problems arise. Leaders of adaptive work encourage people to put conflicting views on the table. They invite participants to talk about disagreements, rather than to hide them or pretend they do not exist.

As we will see in Chapter 8, a group's genuine commitment to an eventual solution depends on an open environment in which people can explore contrasting and competing perspectives. Only when the underlying logic of each side of an argument is laid bare can participants truly understand and make use of the valuable knowledge and experience inherent in competing views. In the process of implementing the adaptive component of a solution, leaders must resist the temptation to provide answers. After conceptualizing the problem, they should encourage workers to do the work they do best. Sharing knowledge in the spirit of collective learning, which requires the capacities to listen and suspend negative judgment, will bring about the commitment essential to reaching a solution.

An excellent example of adaptive leadership was demonstrated by Ralph Larsen when he took the helm of Johnson & Johnson, the $28 billion health care giant based in New Brunswick, New Jersey. The year was 1989, a time when a host of new competitors were recognizing the opportunities in health care. In addition, health care costs around the world seemed to be increasing by the minute, a situation that, as Larsen knew, could not continue indefinitely. Determined to avoid becoming a sleeping giant, Larsen literally made it his first order of business to challenge the company to adapt to the competitive realities.

The change of command occurred at the annual meeting in April 1989. In his first address as chief executive officer, Larsen extolled J&J's past accomplishments, but wasted no time in expressing the need for the company to guard against complacency. What Larsen saw at J&J was not an uncommon ailment: Enormously successful, highly profitable companies often fall prey to their own success. Staffed by the best and the brightest and used to being on top, they begin to believe that they can do no wrong. Indeed, it is exactly this narcissistic mindset that makes such companies so vulnerable when competition heats up or discontinuities appear. Larsen was determined to prevent complacency, born of past success, from smothering Johnson & Johnson's future, and he focused the organization on growth.

Unlike any other *Fortune* 500 company, J&J conducts its business through an astounding number of operating companies— 190 at last count—in fifty-one countries around the world. The managers of its various operating units are so autonomous that they have been referred to as "the kings of their own companies." This uniquely decentralized structure, which has obviously worked well for Johnson & Johnson, presented an unusual obstacle to Larsen's directive for growth. Greater internal competitiveness coupled with a commitment to interdependent partnering were needed. "We wanted to protect and value decentralization," Larsen told me later when we talked in his New Brunswick office.

With his white hair, big frame, and affable manner, Larsen exudes strength and confidence. Decentralization, Larsen continued, "gives ownership and freedom and the ability to move on one's own. Having said that, we needed leaders who recognized that there is strength in the larger corporation . . . if they can help their brother or sister in another part of the business, or they can receive help, they ought to be able to go and do that." How to accomplish that duality of purpose was the key issue. What followed was a remarkable journey of learning and unlearning among the 90,000 people gathered under the Johnson & Johnson corporate umbrella around the world.

Moving quickly to address his own questions as he simultaneously worked to gain broad organizational support for his initiatives, Larsen instituted a series of executive conferences, which brought together 700 senior executives. Rarely were senior managers from J&J's far-flung operations involved in corporate issues. The feeling had long been that if these managers focused on running their own businesses, J&J would take care of itself. But now they were asked to analyze a proprietary case, laying out the corporation's strengths and weaknesses in great detail. Managers, also exposed to performance measures, were shown numbers indicating where Johnson & Johnson stood in relation to approximately two dozen pharmaceutical and consumer product companies. The numbers were shocking. For the first time, the senior executives realized that J&J was being out-performed on most critical measures.

A host of problematic issues and suggestions for dealing with them emerged from Executive Conference I, which ran from eighteen to twenty-four months. Most of the issues were directed back to the executive committee. Convinced of the seriousness of the situation facing J&J, the executive team was committed to taking whatever measures were necessary for solving the problems. Adding to the company's sense of urgency were the Clinton administration's moves to reform health care.

The next step for Johnson & Johnson was to organize a strategy for realizing Larsen's ambition of turning the organization into a "growth company." A skull session with the executive committee developed to remedy ideas that would not destroy J&J's autonomous culture. The committee agreed on the need for more processes and better tracking of information to improve performance measures. Most important, Larsen and his team recognized that they could not solve problems for the individual operating entities. It was time for Executive Conference II, which gave the work back to those who could do it.

This time, the 700 managers were mobilized to define and shape the future of J&J. They were asked to address questions such as: Where should J&J be headed as a corporation? Where should its focus be? What businesses should it should be involved in? What opportunities currently exist for it? How should we deal with its higher-than-average cost structure? "We turned it right back" to the operating companies, explained Larsen. "If you're the managing director in Thailand, or Singapore, or Malaysia, our future [as a corporate entity] is in your hands. This is your business," he told the leaders. "The objective [was] to create an organization that [was] very adaptive, that [was] comparing itself and equipping itself to not only understand the future and what changes are required, but, in fact, to then sort out how will they change the organization," Larsen added. A great deal of communication was fostered through executive committee meetings and the organizationwide conference series, which invited speakers from outside J&J.

Designed to move Larsen's initiative forward, the communication meetings steered people toward examining "competitiveness." Simultaneously, the conferences rejuvenated the process of quality improvement, which began five years earlier in the operating companies, but had never been endorsed as a corporatewide goal. By adopting the language of quality management at the highest corporate levels, Larsen sent a signal to the operating entities that it was time for the entire organization to take the initiative seriously.

This corporate commitment led to what became known as the Signature of Quality (SOQ) program, a linchpin of Larsen's growth-with-quality effort. Larsen considered the program so important that he elevated its leader to the position of corporate staff vice president. The SOQ program, credited with helping the organization "as a whole" learn how to measure performance and improve processes, was developed by members of Larsen's team in a brainstorming session.

Larsen understands the power of emotions and provoking his employees' competitive natures and sense of pride. Johnson & Johnson's Bill Nielsen recalls that at one worldwide conference, the chief executive of another pharmaceutical company, a guest speaker, bluntly criticized J&J's lack of competitiveness within the industry: "He had a great style, and was very provocative. It made me mad as hell!"

Larsen admits to being a leader who, at first blush, often reacts emotionally to problems, but he waits until he has the opportunity to reckon calmly and thoughtfully with a situation before making any decisions. This way, he expresses his feelings openly, but does not allow those feelings to inappropriately affect his business decisions.

Another important aspect of the overall growth initiative at J&J was something known as FrameworkS, deliberately spelled with a capital "S" at the end to denote the multiple "frames" through which an issue can be viewed. Developed by Larsen and his executive committee in the early 1990s in response to the health care reform movement, FrameworkS fostered the notion of participatory management by bringing people from various disciplines together on an expanded executive committee. The executive committee, in turn, became a much more effective decision-making body because its new members offered firsthand knowledge of issues relating to innovations in technology, global markets, and the impact of those issues on various J&J operating companies. Too often, top management is isolated from and ignorant of a company's deeper problems—a danger particularly pronounced in a decentralized structure like that at Johnson & Johnson. To counteract this, FrameworkS facilitated cross-sector cooperation, which turned out to be critical to the growth initiative as a whole. FrameworkS' success deserves more attention, and I will discuss it further in Chapter 4.

Equally important for Larsen to achieve his ambition for growth with quality was a shared system of values within the organization's culture. From the beginning, Larsen strongly emphasized the importance of a value system based on the Johnson & Johnson credo. The credo, a 308-word code of ethics in which customers are the highest priority, begins this way: "We believe our first responsibility is to the doctors, nurses, and patients, and to the mothers and fathers." So important is the credo to the Johnson & Johnson culture that a copy of it is carved in stone at the company's New Brunswick headquarters. Still, the values were not always respected. A series of embarrassing incidents in the early 1990s—shredding documents during a federal investigation of off-label drug promotion, and a penalty for willful patent violation, to name two—prompted Larsen to institute "challenge" sessions. Every executive attended a two-day course on the meaning of the credo and how it should affect decisions. At one of the worldwide management conferences, Nielsen recalls Larsen speaking forcefully against such reprehensible behavior, making it clear that illegal or inappropriate actions would not be condoned under any circumstances, and he made it everyone's responsibility to put a stop to it. "That's not what we're about," Larsen told his troops. At the end of his remarks, he received a standing ovation. Shortly thereafter, Nielsen reports, a few people who realized they did not fit into Larsen's vision for J&J decided to leave.

It has been more than a decade since Ralph Larsen set Johnson & Johnson on a course designed to make it more competitive in the changing world of health care. The numbers reveal how the company has responded to his challenge. J&J's pretax profit margin increased from 15.5 percent in 1988 to 21.3 percent in 1998, whereas the net profit margin climbed from 10.8 percent to 15.5 percent. The ten-year return to shareholders comes in at a healthy 25.2 percent, compounded annually. That means that $10,000 invested in J&J at the end of 1988 grew to $95,000 a decade later. A look behind the profit numbers shows a company that has managed to increase its spending on research-and-development by more than 300 percent over the last decade, to $2.3 billion in 1998 from only $700 million in 1988. Adroitly positioned for the future, Johnson & Johnson underwent a dramatic shift in its allocation of businesses. What it calls "knowledge-based businesses"—its pharmaceutical and professional segments—account for nearly three-quarters of sales today, compared to 59 percent a decade ago.

Enlightened leaders like Ralph Larsen recognize that the best ideas for a solution's adaptive approach emerge from the minds and experiences of their employees. Good leaders strive to help others develop into leaders, too. "*The Prince of Egypt* model of leadership—here's the plan, follow me, I'll take you to the promised land—is out," says Jonathan Bulkeley, chief executive officer of New York–based Barnesandnoble.com, Inc. He writes in *Fast Company* that "in a business environment where the clock is ticking faster than ever, it's not the job of leaders to have all the answers." Bulkeley's job, in his hybrid world of online book selling, is not simply to recruit book buyers. Rather, he must identify the company's problems, and then, in his words, "find and develop people who are relentless about asking, 'Why does the publishing business work this way?' and who are confident about demanding, 'What were we thinking? We need to change now.'" In other words, Bulkeley, like Ralph Larsen, encourages his employees to take leadership roles: that is, to pose pertinent questions and envision workable answers. Only by developing a cadre of involved, committed employees can Bulkeley hope to successfully execute the strategy that will put Barnesandnoble.com in the Internet winners' circle.

Here are some of the questions leaders pose to themselves and their employees, as part of the adaptive component of a solution.

Ask yourself . . .

- What deeply held beliefs could blind us to the future, both as individuals and as a collective unit?
- What new learning is needed?
- What unlearning has to take place if we are to realize our ambitions?
- How ready are we to undertake that unlearning?

- What competing values are at stake?

Ralph Larsen's success over the past decade at Johnson & Johnson exemplifies a successful execution of my leadership framework. He understands intuitively that technical and adaptive work is unlikely to be created and implemented in neat, separate programs. Applying technical change in the form of performance benchmarking, he jolted employees out of their complacency and skillfully focused their attention on growth. At the same time, he used adaptive measures, such as Signature of Quality and FrameworkS, to change the organization's culture.

Next

As the chapters that follow show, my four-part leadership framework can greatly simplify the leader's job, which, of course, does not mean that complex and extremely difficult decisions are avoided. In fact, leaders must attend to the hardest work: mobilizing an entire workforce to adapt to major changes and to participate in solving the problems that confront their organizations.

My seven essential acts of leadership, which are the subject of part two, will help you in this undertaking by laying out the real work of leaders quite specifically, in easily understood components. I begin with a brief explanation of each act in the next chapter.

PART TWO

A Leader's Real Work

3

The Seven Essential Acts of Leadership

THE COMFORT OF FAMILIARITY can be a seductive trap. Just ask Jason Olim, cofounder, president, and chief executive officer of CDNow, Inc., a $100-million-a-year music retailer based in Fort Washington, Pennsylvania. Twenty-nine-year-old Olim started the company with his twin brother, Matthew, in the basement of their parents' home. He describes unlearning what he calls "the infamous entrepreneur's mantra: If you don't do it, it won't get done right. As CEO," he writes in *Fast Company*, "I've learned that my role is less about what I can do and more about what the organization can do. That fundamental change in my beliefs led to a fundamental change in my behavior."

Olim now resists the urge to barrel straight into a crisis, roll up his sleeves, and tell everyone else what to do. "I now wait for the people involved to come tell me their solution," he confesses in his article. But it took a less-than-gentle nudge from his brother to turn Olim around. "My own brother forbade me to modify a piece of code that I'd written to re-size the album-

43

cover graphics on the company's Web site," Olim remembers. As chief of the company's technology group, Olim's brother told him he "had no right to disturb his team's process." Today, Olim readily admits that his brother was right, but still recalls it was "a hard pill to swallow."

Because taking action can lead to a sense of accomplishment, leaders may be tempted to immerse themselves in problems that they already know how to resolve. In doing so, leaders neglect the very complexities that they alone can untangle. Overlooking such issues, as Olim discovered, may result in dire consequences for the organization.

However adroitly one manages to rationalize resolving a comfortably familiar dilemma instead of addressing leadership's real business, at some point a leader must cease performing others' work and assume executive responsibilities. Each of the seven essential acts of leadership suggests a productive approach for helping to do just that.

The acts, which are introduced below, are discussed in greater detail in the chapters that follow. The acts include a call for leaders to "get on the balcony," communicate what is real, clarify conflicting values, promote dialogue among workers, relieve workers' distress whenever possible, and emphasize the concept of collective responsibility. In the epilogue, I discuss the importance of finding meaningful solutions.

Get on the Balcony

A leader must be able to see far and wide, as though standing aloft a high balcony with the capacity to view every aspect of the business and the marketplace in which it operates. Consciously imposing a distance between oneself and the company's daily activities is necessary to avoid the temptation of becoming overly involved in those duties. Despite the fact that they have climbed onto the balcony, purposeful leaders never lose sight of or interest in developments below them.

Indeed, effective leaders play dual roles in the corporate drama: They are involved in many aspects of the company's daily operations and at the same time they think about routine activities within the context of the company's overall performance. This multilayered perspective is not always easy to maintain, but unless leaders develop this capacity, their companies will flounder. I intend, in this balcony metaphor, to encourage leaders to establish a balance between contemplation and action by moving freely back and forth between the balcony and the field. In this way, they resist the temptation of working myopically with familiar and comfortable operational details and enable themselves to sustain their far-sighted vision of an entire company working toward growth.

Communicate What Is Real

Asked about the overall context of their companies, employees are often confused. They know (or should know) precisely what is expected of them during daily routines. Few realize, however, where an individual job interfaces with the totality of the company's functions, which is especially problematic when leaders are guiding their companies into new territory. Leaders count on loyalty from their employees, but they must inspire allegiance by conveying a sense of shared common interest in the company to their workers. This is always important, but most crucial at times of change. The newest responsibility of leaders is to explain what's going on—to everyone. That is, leaders must communicate simply, fully, and clearly how they view the company's ultimate aim—its ambition—and the context in which that ambition will be achieved.

Only then can leaders expect employees to share in their perceptions and to support their plans for the future.

Clarify Competing Values

Although values are amorphous entities, they can still be shared. Indeed, shared values are the backbone of societies, cultures, and organizations. Certainly, it is not easy for everyone to share the same values. Differences in work experiences, attitudes, goals, and aspirations result in different values. Deliberately using the term "differences" to denote no intrinsic value, I emphasize the inappropriateness of judging others' values when the shared goal is to address a specific problem.

Different values turn into competing or conflicting values when situations change, but attitudes do not. For example, when leaders decide to change the company's direction and embark on a new course, they may confront colleagues and employees who disagree. If the leader expects to progress, he or she must identify opposing individuals and help each one to understand the thought processes underlying the proposal for change. Aiming to help people discover and adapt to new ways of thinking and working, the leader should quickly address the concerns of ambivalent employees because lingering doubt will cause distress for everyone. As I said, shared values are the heart and backbone of a company.

Support Changes in Values

Constant reinforcement of the new set of values is imperative. But sometimes, in the midst of implementing measures for adaptive change, leaders confront a troubling but interesting dilemma: At the same time the company is working toward establishing a new set of values that hopefully will invigorate its long-term performance, a crisis arises in which a return to the old value system appears to be the solution. What is the best thing to do?

Stand firm in favor of the values you are in the process of instilling throughout the organization. Reverting to the former system (even once) disheartens employees and promotes cynicism, because it signifies a betrayal of principles. Cultural transformation is always a daunting task; the leader's clarity of purpose, combined with his or her capacity to communicate that purpose so that it becomes a shared goal, is the best way to effect crucial companywide adherence to a common set of principles. Any indication that a leader is not completely committed to the new agenda is the death knell for a solution that requires adaptive work. However, if competing *positive* values, ideas not born simply from a regressive wish to avoid change, are suggested, they certainly should be examined thoroughly. Doing so will provide valuable insight as well as promote shared acceptance of the course eventually chosen. To give consideration to competing values reflects appropriate thoroughness and bears no resemblance to waffling.

Promote Dialogue

Even during the iciest days of the Cold War, Americans and Russians continued talking to each other, and even occasionally agreed on an issue. Whenever they did, international tensions lessened and hopes for peace strengthened. In fact, many historians argue that conversations between these two great powers may have saved us from a third world war because dialogue represents more than an attempt to argue the correctness of a strongly held position. Dialogue advances learning and understanding. Comprehending the logic underlying a competing position often removes one's resistance to accepting it. Dialogue can smooth the way when a leader wants to initiate an adaptive solution. Since there are always (at least) two sides to an issue, leaders must work to explain and clarify their positions by focusing on discussions of the issues at hand. At all costs, these discussions must be participatory so that each employee feels his or her voice has been heard.

Regulate Distress

Implementing an adaptive component of a solution is not a tranquil passage to the future. It can even be painful. On one hand, the pain and pressure that accompany major changes in business, as in life, can reach a level of distress at which productive functioning is inhibited. On the other hand, workers who are altogether unaware or unaffected by profound transformations surrounding them may be equally unproductive.

Therefore, leaders must diligently watch the level of distress among workers and maneuver a balance between too much and not enough. In Chapter 9 I will discuss how skilled leaders develop a capacity for managing distress like a pressure cooker, turning up the heat slowly, allowing enough steam to escape safely, to avoid an explosion.

Make Everyone Collectively Responsible

Responsibility is a two-way street. The leader, recognizing the need to facilitate opportunities in which employees can assume responsibilities, must follow through by actually giving work back to those who can do it. Employees in whose bailiwick a problem resides must be *willing* to accept accountability for solving it and the leader needs to assess workers' attitudes toward assuming it. In other words, attitude carries as much weight as action. It isn't always an easy journey, no matter which direction one comes from. Wise leaders realize that everyone gains when responsibility is distributed appropriately throughout a company. Although insights are exchanged up and down the corporate ladder, frontline employees' antennae often detect market changes and growth opportunities long before these subtleties reach the stratosphere of the chief executive. This is an advantage of being close to the customers. Leaders who have grown beyond the old command-and-control stratagems of managing and who encourage their employees to take responsibility will reap rewards. Their employees, motivated to do their best, will do so, learning to voice ideas and use their initiative.

The book concludes with a discussion on creating "meaning." Shakespeare described "meaning" in *King Lear* with the phrase "Ripeness is all." It is the exuberance that comes to anyone wholly engaged in a good cause or possessing the wealth, not of money or possessions, but of living life fully, with all one's senses and sympathies intact. It is the pleasure of creating something new and astonishing. Meaning is living and growing.

My approach calls for distributing responsibilities throughout the ranks, but it should not be confused with that much-used term, "empowerment." Burdened with negative connotations, the term is unpopular with business audiences, because it invokes "soft" or impractical ideas predicated on the notion that workers should, as a matter of principle, have *complete* autonomy in the workplace.

To my mind, there are four familiar myths about empowerment that require debunking. The first is that given proper authority, frontline people and their managers will do the right thing for the customer. I remember listening on a headset while a customer services representative at a company that makes workstations responded to calls. (Customer service is the next point of call when neither the frontline worker nor manager can solve a problem.) This time, the consumer complained that her machine had broken down three times in the past year, and she wanted it replaced. The conversation went back and forth until the representative exercised his authority to refuse her request, leaving a very dissatisfied customer. He turned to me and said, "She didn't have a leg to stand on" in seeking a replacement, adding, "That product usually needs to be repaired six times a year."

As my friend and longtime colleague, Yves Doz, likes to say, "People moving from highly controlled environments to so-called empowered ones frequently behave like delinquents."

The second myth is that people want to be empowered. Not necessarily so. I know many senior executives who have attempted to "empower" their employees, only to be told, "I would prefer the rules." As far as I know, surveyed workers have never asked for more authority, even in their own area of responsibility. Most workers and managers are more comfortable functioning within a prescribed set of rules.

The third myth is that empowerment and control are mutually exclusive. "You need both," John Nordstrom, chairman and chief executive officer of Nordstrom, Inc., told me. "We give individual salespeople and department managers wide authority in dealing with the customer. This is supported by a regional management reporting system that relates performance to sales per hour and compares departments to other stores in the region and across the nation." Anyone who shops at Nordstrom is aware of the wide discretion the sales force has in dealing with customers. Salespeople are empowered to make on-the-spot decisions regarding product returns and replacements; they can accompany a customer from department to department, developing a relationship along the way; salespeople have their own customer lists and know shoppers by name. Most important, salespeople are familiar with their customers' tastes and buying styles and are always looking for new items that might suit them.

Employees performing within the Nordstrom model of empowerment and control can earn five or six times the industry average, reports John Nordstrom. But it is not a system designed for everyone. The performance measurement system, which makes employee rankings public to coworkers, is too stressful for some people.

The final myth I want to challenge is the erroneous belief that workers must be empowered to be responsive to customers. We can look at aspects of the airline industry to illustrate my point.

The pilot is a professional, but his "freedom" to make decisions is limited. Adhering precisely to procedure, he is required to perform specific checks prior to a flight, and follow standard rules if problems arise during the flight. I doubt that customers would want it otherwise. Imagine how you would feel if you overheard the pilot saying to his copilot, "Instead of using 3,500 feet of runway for takeoff at 160 miles per hour, let's see if we can get this sucker up in the air in 2,000 feet at 200 miles per hour." The flight attendant also has the power to improvise regarding passengers' comfort, but certainly not regarding safety requirements. Yet the employees' restrictions do not impact passenger service.

I give the final word on empowerment to Peter Bijur, chairman and chief executive officer of Texaco, whose views, expressed in a conversation with me a few years ago, mirror my own.

I want people to think and take responsibility, but I also want to make a distinction between empowerment and democracy. I am very disciplined about the delegation of authority. People should follow the rules and regulations—if you want to change these, come to see me with a compelling reason for the change. Make mistakes, yes, but I expect people to correct mistakes in areas they have the authority to act.

Next

When leaders become so immersed in the daily running and minor crises of their companies that they remain unaware of their organization's need for strategic redirection, they are risking the future of the entire corporation.

In the following chapter, I relate the stories of business leaders who, accurately perceiving impending danger, stepped back from operational details to evaluate the company in its entirety. Doing so enabled them to restructure priorities, recast the company's strategy, and lead their corporations away from the brink of failure to the safety of solid success.

4

Stand Back and See

MY FRIEND RON HEIFETZ once said that the true heroism of leadership involves having the courage to face reality and the capacity to help the people around you do the same. Long before strategies are laid out, budgets are set, or plans are implemented, leaders must search for and find the true circumstances that they and their organizations face. Larry Bossidy, who spent thirty-four years at General Electric before joining AlliedSignal, has described effective leaders as those who come to "a brutal understanding of reality" before they determine a specific strategy.

Encountering harsh realities is among the most difficult tasks that a leader will face. One can only imagine how painful it was for Lewis E. Platt, a more than thirty-year veteran of Palo Alto, California–based Hewlett-Packard, to recognize the necessity of breaking apart his giant enterprise. To his credit, he did so, to the advantage of all concerned.

Frequently, a company confronts problems in the present because it is attempting to adhere to paradigms of management that it has grown beyond. If this happens, leaders have to contemporize these frameworks so they are, once again, relevant.

The difficulty, however, lies in the fact that, previously, these outmoded or constricting guidelines had been extremely useful, perhaps even formative in the company's development. I asked Lew Platt how he steers HP away from stagnating elements, especially when they were, up until now, deeply satisfying and rewarding. In fact, my blunt inquiry was, "How do you bury the past?" Admitting that the past style of management was "wonderful . . . for a much less complicated sub-billion-dollar company, it doesn't necessarily work for a much more complicated $40 billion company." In fact, Platt suspects that a key reason why so many organizations "hit the growth wall" is that their leaders' views on management fail to advance and expand as the company does so.

Anticipating a hard truth, Jack Welch at General Electric refused to be left behind. In this case, Welch reacted to an influx of foreign competition by restructuring his company's operations so they could meet the challenge of new competition. He once said: "The best way to play your hand is to face reality—see the world the way it is—and act accordingly." Frequently, this is more difficult than it sounds.

Sometimes, facing realities can feel impossible. A leader that stays in tune with the daily flow of the company's enterprises, stays in contact with people on the front line and in the back office, and oversees the proper execution of strategies at the same time as remaining separate from these concerns may feel as though he or she must overcome the laws of nature to be in several places at once. Although leaders are involved with these concerns, they need to withdraw and stand apart from them, too. Leaders must be free to see the whole picture, even if that view is unpleasant, and this entails focusing a sharp eye on shifts in technology and relevant market changes. It is critical for leaders to be fully aware of how each element of their organizations intersects with (or fails to intersect with) other elements. Leaders need the capacity to remain involved with routine matters and outside them, concurrently.

The same ability contributes to what makes sports figures legendary, like basketball's Earvin "Magic" Johnson and hockey's Bobby Orr. Able to survey the entire playing field as they participated in the game, both Johnson and Orr consistently displayed their abilities both to score points or goals and to observe the game's larger patterns. In other words, each kept the entire game as well as his individual role in it in mind. On the other hand, average players are so focused on the action of the moment that they are blind to the big picture and, as a result, miss out on major opportunities because they fail to notice who is open for a pass, who has missed a block, or who is in a position to score.

In today's quicksilver business world, leaders would do well to learn from Magic Johnson and Bobby Orr. If we think about Kenneth P. Olsen, the ill-fated founder of Digital Equipment Corporation (DEC), who did so well stealing away IBM's mainframe customers but failed to notice the emerging personal-computer business, we realize that he was extremely, and, as it turned out, inappropriately focused on one issue. "Who would ever want a computer on [his or her] desk?" Olsen is said to have asked dismissively before vetoing a proposal to build a PC in the 1970s. "There is no reason for individuals to have computers in their homes," he famously continued. When millions of computer-hungry consumers came up with just as many reasons for home computers, DEC began to slide into an abyss—and Olsen was asked to leave his own corporation. Although he was a gifted engineer and leader, Olsen's myopic view of the market prevented him from seeing the realities in the future. No matter how hard we try, we all have blind spots.

Speaking ironically of business leaders such as Olsen, who emphatically declare to "know" their markets, only to have those markets "move away from them . . . largely undetected," Larry Bossidy considers the "primary challenge" of leadership to be the creation of "a culture in which people focus on where they are going, instead of where they have been." Great players observe the flow of the game, watching how offense and defense work together. Having a broader perspective—what I call the "view from the balcony"—these players become the team's leaders, because they are more conscious of what is taking place at every level of the game and, therefore, able to make better plays.

Although several reasons explain why business leaders may spend too much time solving everyday, operational problems when they should be climbing the stairs to the balcony, a common one is that many honestly believe that they can ill afford the time *not* to oversee routine matters. The sum of the operating choices becomes the strategy. They get sucked into time-consuming operational problems at the expense of strategic thinking. Often, I have been in day-long meetings where the first half of the day was intended for operating issues, and the second for strategy, but the operating issues carried the day. So they seek information relevant only to their immediate problems and ultimately make major unenlightened decisions without comprehending the realities of the business's larger needs. The real tragedy is that, when this happens, leaders are doing the work that people below them should be doing and *not* focusing on the work people within the organization are counting on them, and only them, to do.

To be worthy of the description, leaders must proficiently move back and forth between the field and the balcony, constantly assessing which offers a view more vital to the organization's welfare at any given moment.

In an organization as large as Johnson & Johnson which, as I pointed out in Chapter 2, is a $28-billion-a-year enterprise, comprised of more than 190 distinct operating companies, many leaders, not just one, must be prepared to take deep breaths and climb to the balcony. Founded in 1887, Johnson & Johnson has survived for more than a century. The central question now is how it can remain nimble, flexible, and responsive to whatever occurs in a complex and ambiguous business world. "From where we sit at Johnson & Johnson," Ralph Larsen once wrote, "the twenty-first century holds only one certainty: the prospect of an ever more dizzying pace of change." Though Larsen thought otherwise, conventional business wisdom dictates that as a company gets bigger, it needs to slow its growth. When he took the helm at the pharmaceutical company in 1989, however, he realized that the long-held belief would prove true unless J&J could overcome the problems inherent in its unorthodox structure. At the same time, it had to confront head-on the realities of a changing competitive landscape.

Evaluating how the entire organization could become and remain apprised of the problems and challenges it faced as a whole became an early priority for Larsen. How could he motivate the leaders of its widely dispersed individual operating companies to embrace a unified perspective, which was necessary for J&J to continue to grow? A deeply rooted sense of ownership within the individual companies can be both a tremendous strength and an enormous problem, Larsen admitted. It presents what I call a "learning disability" for leaders who are in the process of implementing an adaptive solution. Despite the stumbling blocks of varied geographies, organizations, and functions, Larsen and his executive committee resolved to overcome any obstacle in the path of achieving a consistent, cohesive, and growth-oriented enterprise. After all, they had no other choice. "Despite our massive size," Larsen says, "we have to be more competent at adapting our companies to all kinds of change, or [we] risk becoming irrelevant."

What emerged from management's commitment was a dramatic and innovative approach to problem solving, the process the company calls *FrameworkS*, which I introduced in Chapter 2. Larsen explained that J&J "wanted to achieve a kind of 'framework' through which [we could] better understand where we stood in our markets, what people expected of us, how we could be more responsive, and how we could identify new opportunities for growth and development. The capital 'S' ending FrameworkS signifies the multiple 'frames' through which we must view our diverse businesses." The company wanted to take advantage of perhaps its richest resource—the experience and expertise available within each operating company. In addition, Larsen and his team worked to counteract what they perceived to be the inward focus of the organization. People had to become more responsive to the outside world.

As part of the FrameworkS process, the company invites ten to twelve people from the corporate sphere to be temporary members of the usually nine-member executive committee. Chosen for the geographic, technical, or organizational perspectives they can contribute toward resolving the immediate issue, the group may include an operations manager from McNeil, a product manager from Janssen, and an information-technology expert from a corporation. These are not high-ranking executives; rather, they are people with the ability to bring diversity and add value to the discussion. Then, Larsen and his expanded executive committee go to a remote location, such as Sea Island, Georgia, where the group isolates itself for a full week— that's right, a week, not an afternoon or day or weekend—to address the problem at hand. The meetings are run democratically, so no one asserts rank and no opinion carries more weight than another. The expanded executive committee then decides what steps need to be taken.

From this initial gathering, subcommittees and task forces are organized, each with a mandate to research and investigate a particular topic. Eventually, hundreds of people throughout the corporation have input on decisions that will affect the entire corporation. In essence, Ralph Larsen is bringing several employees onto the balcony with him, thus widening the Johnson & Johnson panorama in previously unimagined ways. As a successful example of the FrameworkS process, a J&J team went to Japan to strengthen the company's position in that market. Astonishingly, the team proposed about 1,000 possibilities.

Research teams study analyses of operating procedures, as well as overall policies and specific practices. The results are evaluated by the FrameworkS team and the executive committee. Next, FrameworkS management teams design a plan of action based on the earlier research and discussion.

Ten FrameworkS teams have instituted initiatives whose outlines became clear to the managers only after their experiences of climbing onto and understanding the view from the balcony. As a result, the company has entered new markets, founded new businesses, established programs in technology and recruitment, and, of course, encouraged innovation. Simultaneously, the company has paid overdue attention to leadership development. Larsen refers to FrameworkS as "a proven means of releasing energy throughout the corporation and focusing the eyes of the organization and its leadership on the two most important issues central to our future—innovation and change." He describes a FrameworkS initiative, which could take six months, as not only exacting, but requiring "a significant additional commitment of time and energy from people who already hold some of the most demanding positions in our company." Although it may not be the only solution to the company's problems, FrameworkS is ideally suited to the unique structure of J&J.

Here are two particularly interesting initiatives that emerged from FrameworkS task forces. The first, on the topic of "leadership," is a program developed in FrameworkS 6. "Standards of leadership" is the company's first formal "attempt at expressing the essential values [that] . . . should represent the profile of current and future leaders of this organization." In August 1996, that month's issue of FrameworkS' newsletter announced that this important effort yielded "a uniform evaluation technique that can serve as a guide for our operating units in recruiting and succession planning."

Emerging from FrameworkS 9, "What's New?" is a program that aims "to transform [J&J] into a place where people ask, 'what's new?' and think about innovative ways of doing things as often as they ask 'how's business?'" If the question "'how's business?' implies a focus on past actions and a priority on the bottom line, 'what's new?' puts the emphasis on what people are doing to achieve target growth rates and to strengthen competitiveness." In the same newsletter, Bill Egan, a company executive, expressed his confidence that J&J "can make the meaning of this two-word question a living part of our organization, [resulting in] . . . a lot more innovation in everything we do."

Other companies may opt for a different approach after the leadership concludes that change is vital to the company's survival, but it will always be a choice between action and contemplation. George A. Lorch, chairman, president, and chief executive officer of Armstrong World Industries, Inc. in Lancaster, Pennsylvania, had to make such a choice. In the early 1980s, Lorch found himself wondering why the market valuation of Armstrong, a maker of interior furnishings, was so low. That led him to take off his rose-colored glasses and make the difficult climb to the balcony. From there, he took a hard look at his business as a whole, searching for social patterns, behavior patterns of competitors, and changes in technology; he was searching for anything that might indicate what had gone wrong at Armstrong. From the balcony, Lorch discovered a complacent company avoiding tough choices and blinded by its 135 years of success. Suddenly, he realized that

> The world . . . was changing, and we just weren't competitive. In our businesses, we create careful strategies for organizational survival, but we often don't notice (or choose to ignore) how quickly the facts governing our strategies begin to change. Change is unforgiving. It is steady and relentless, and it sweeps past the unaware and the unaccepting, leaving them adrift in the shallows.

In a speech on this subject, Lorch added: "It's a lonely moment, particularly if the company and its culture are what you've grown up with and feel safe in."

Determining that drastic action was the only possible cure, Lorch recognized that Armstrong's best hope for a turnaround lay in concentrating on its core businesses, flooring and building products. The company sold its largest subsidiary, Thomasville Furniture, in 1955 and put its entire textile products business up for sale. From his view on the balcony, Lorch was convinced that the company was top-heavy and slow to make decisions. To remedy this, other operations were restructured and many jobs were lost. When it was all over, however, an underperforming company began to mark record sales, and its stock price rose by 61 percent.

After climbing to the balcony, George Lorch saw what he had to do, as did Jan Carlzon, the legendary president and chief executive officer of Scandinavian Airline Systems. Both men have what Carlzon has called "helicopter sense"—that is, "a talent for rising above the details to see the lay of the land," or what I have been referring to as "getting on the balcony." Certainly the term is less important than the concept, which expresses a broad-range perspective, an overview of a company's past, present, and future. In adaptive work, the key is to see social patterns and competing views, not just the business standpoint.

Carlzon was appointed chief operating officer of SAS in 1980, a time when the entire airline industry was in a slump following the oil crisis of the 1970s, when oil-producing nations sharply curtailed shipments and fuel prices skyrocketed. Even SAS, profitable for seventeen consecutive years, was facing its second year in the red. Since Carlzon's reputation as a cost cutter preceded him, his colleagues at SAS expected fare reductions, expense reductions, or both. But the experienced executive knew that the circumstances at SAS were different.

Carlzon needed a view from the balcony in order to discern patterns in the company's behavior and to learn about its culture and values and how its former leaders had dealt with previous crises. Analyzing the organization's history, Carlzon was surprised to discover a company so weakened by his predecessor's unsuccessful attempts to remain competitive that it had become unable to provide services that would satisfy customers. Until the oil crisis, SAS had been "flying high" in a stable market with little competition. When the market stagnated, managers slashed costs, and did so by cutting equally across all departments. Unfortunately, the reductions did more than trim unneeded fat; they also hacked away at the services customers wanted and expected. In addition, because it had lowered morale, cost cutting had actually harmed the carrier's ability to compete. Carlzon knew that further cuts were out of the question and decided the solution lay in boosting sales.

Still on the balcony, he planned a strategy to make SAS "the best airline in the world for the frequent business traveler," who almost always pays full fare, and whose trips, for most airlines, account for about 6 percent of the passengers, but 47 percent of sales. Moreover, business travelers make their trips regardless of the condition of the economy. Part of the strategy aimed to give work back to those who could do it best and imbue appropriate employees with more authority and responsibility. Carlzon got on the balcony and decided to pursue the business traveler with a gusto unmatched by his competitors. The single-mindedness of Carlzon's strategy distinguished his abilities, as well as his implementation, which required stepping down from the balcony and onto the field of action.

Before we join him on the field, let us look at how the SAS saga operates within my framework. Remember, the framework simplifies the leader's work by categorizing problems as either operational or strategic. Next, it identifies the technical and adaptive components of solutions. After ascending the balcony, Jan Carlzon realized that the airline's goals and, indeed, its entire culture, including chain of command, needed to be thoroughly reconceptualized. Since the problems were not operational alone, Carlzon's proposed solution included more than technical changes. The solution's adaptive aspect asked nothing less of each employee than to change his or her focus and manner of operating, as well as to shoulder more responsibility for problem solving.

First, Carlzon and his management team examined the company's procedures and expenditures to assess their value within the new strategy of catering to business travelers. A few specific changes included a decision to ground SAS's highly touted and recently acquired Airbuses. He literally sent the planes to a desert location until they could be sold or applied to other routes. These planes have 335 seats and are very hard to fill to capacity, so they make only one round trip a day between London and Stockholm, a schedule that would not attract business travelers. He won the board of directors' approval for an additional $45 million and raised operating expenses by $12 million a year. He organized courses on improving services, upgraded the Copenhagen hub, and committed the airline to on-time flight performance, whenever possible. Carlzon eliminated first class and in its place instituted EuroClass, a full-fare section primarily for business travelers. My point is that every detail, no matter how minor, was examined and considered.

Going to the balcony gave Carlzon the perspective he needed to uncover the actual patterns that contributed to SAS's misfortunes. Specifically, he looked for problems in systems as well as in social and behavioral patterns among employees. Revealing troubled areas, he devised a solution that took advantage of SAS's considerable human resources by shifting the locus of responsibility to the front line.

How Does One Stand Back and See?

How do successful leaders go about the task of comprehending and confronting reality? In my years of work and research in this area, I have observed a number of techniques that address the question. Primary among them is:

Adopt Your Customers' Perspective

In the automobile industry, the Saturn Corporation, based in Spring Hill, Tennessee, bears the standard as a customer-oriented company. From its inception, Saturn defined itself as a customer service enterprise. Traditionally, car companies have focused their primary efforts on selling their products' design and engine power. But Saturn, a subsidiary of General Motors, decided to identify with the customer's experience of buying a car. The company sought out the unmet, unserved needs of its customers and experimented with alternative solutions. And this resulted in an entirely new approach. Saturn reviewed all the ways in which customers communicate with the company, after which it redesigned each and every communication. For example, haggling over price was eliminated. In addition, customers were made to feel the security that accompanies top-flight service and repairs. Perhaps most interesting, it assured its customers that their perspective motivated all of the company's operations by nurturing a feeling of community among Saturn owners through letters from the company and social gatherings organized by Saturn. Customers have responded in the best way possible: They buy one Saturn after another. In other words, repeat sales represent the customers' loyalty.

Never Stop Asking Questions

Ron Heifetz often urges his Harvard University students to "interrogate reality," by which he means that they must uncover and understand the reasoning that underlies a debate or disagreement. It is not enough simply to know the particular data of a case.

I give the same advice to my clients, and use a well-known story about Xerox Corporation that illustrates the power of understanding underlying rationale. According to the story, the transformation of the company began at an annual shareholders' meeting. Xerox had recently halted production of its 3300 copier, which was supposed to be its answer to low-cost Japanese competitors. When then-chief executive officer David Kearns opened the meeting for questions, a Xerox assembly-line worker, Frank Enos, stepped up to the microphone and expressed his rage at the executive. "We all knew the 3300 was a piece of junk," he told Kearns. "We could have told you. Why didn't you ask us?" Here was a situation in which the unspoken social convention dictating that low-ranking employees do not knock on the chief executive's door to offer advice and vice versa kept the executives unaware of problems that could have been rectified before causing any damage.

To his credit, Kearns resolved to find the solution, not only to the dilemma related to that particular copier, but to the cultural problem that blocked communication between tiers so thoroughly that an enormous problem was hidden from view until it was too late to correct. What he learned was that leaders must maintain open lines of communication with everyone, from the assembly line to the front line. It was a discovery that changed the entire corporation. Later, Kearns was given an opportunity to show his appreciation for his wake-up call from the assembly line. When the U.S. Department of Commerce awarded Xerox a Baldrige National Quality Award, Kearns invited Frank Enos to the ceremony in Washington, D.C.

Still, for some leaders, it is not easy to ask employees for their opinions. This has never been part of their training for the job. In fact, the opposite is true. As Larry Bossidy has pointed out, the traditional hierarchical organization of most corporations has fostered a kind of isolationism that has allowed "talented lone rangers" to rise through the ranks. In such an atmosphere, it is unlikely to find leaders wandering around seeking advice. Moreover, leaders who are successful within such a stratified and isolated system perpetuate it, perhaps unwittingly, because they look to others like themselves for their successors. "All of the learning that led to one kind of success," John Seely Brown of Xerox wrote in *Fast Company,* "works against your ability to unlearn." It is a difficult, but not impossible, task. Brown related how he struggles against deeply ingrained ideas, specifically by seeking out diverse opinions and skills. "My senior team and I have a two-hour lunch every Friday where we reflect on what we did well, what we did wrong, and what we can learn from it all. Some of what is said to me at those meetings isn't too pleasant," he admitted. In the long run, however, Brown knows that a bit of unpleasantness is a small price to pay for the capacity to change your perspective and rethink a situation or a product, or to have a company clear about reality. Again, in Bossidy's words, "Leaders have to be ready to accept honest feedback about their own performance. And the good ones do."

Listen Deeply with Curiosity and Empathy

The next path for leaders to follow is a natural extension of the previous one. To understand the realities confronting their companies, leaders should listen with curiosity and empathy to everyone who can contribute to that understanding.

All the great leaders I have known and worked with are keenly aware that they do not know all the answers or, perhaps, even the best answers. Leaders resist the temptation to assume a more conventional stance of leadership, that of instant problem solver. Instead of answering questions immediately, good leaders will often turn them back to the inquirer to ponder. It is the same technique employed by teachers since Socrates and psychoanalysts since Freud.

Once leaders recognize their limitations as problem solvers, they are more likely to become genuinely empathic listeners who are better fortified to face realities. Realizing and acknowledging limits allows a leader to develop a new kind of curiosity that ultimately enhances her or his problem-solving skills. By definition, leaders who are empathic listeners are able to imagine themselves in the speaker's shoes, and understand reality from a heretofore unexplored perspective.

As leaders work to discern social patterns within their organizations, they may discover that the capacity to listen deeply is their most valuable tool. During any discussion of significant issues, members of the executive team are bound to disagree. If the leader remains extremely attentive to the dynamics within the group—who is bickering with whom, who refuses to cooperate on particular issues, noticing whether the same people always seem to disagree with each other or with the leader—the leader may be able to identify and understand what is underlying the dissension. Perhaps the disagreement is not actually about the issue at hand, but instead stems from personal antagonism between two people who have staked out opposing sides on the initiative as a way of expressing their conflict.

Next

The first act of leaders, then, is to frame their organization's problems by climbing up onto the balcony to get a wide-angle view. From that perspective, they are better able to reflect on the technical and adaptive components that will comprise the appropriate solution.

Climbing to the balcony and facing reality is hard work and frequently stressful, but once there, a leader will be invigorated by recognizing that he or she has finally begun the battle to correct the organization, and there is no turning back. Now the leader's goal is to convey to the company, as a whole, the value of the ambition and why the strategy is worthwhile and, hopefully, workable. I refer to this process as setting the context, and it is the subject of the following chapter.

5

Communicate
What Is Real

L EADERS CAN TAKE NOTHING FOR GRANTED—least of all their employees. Gordon Binder, chairman and chief executive officer of
Amgen, Inc., the large biotechnology company based in Thou-
sand Oaks, California, has said that he believes that "the boss's
primary job is to help his subordinates do their jobs. It's not their
primary job to help him do his." Binder is right; nonetheless,
employees at many companies are being asked to know the
business as well as its owners. These companies complain that
because the employees now have stock options, "they should
have a different perspective." What such companies fail to understand is the enormous difference between distributing
shares and changing how people think.

Employees cannot be expected to integrate new information
and concepts unless leaders properly orient them to the assumptions they are expected to share. In other words, leaders
must set the context, which means they are obligated to clarify
their ambition, explain the strategies necessary to achieve it,
and point out how this proposed path differs from those traveled

in the past. Most important, leaders need to translate the "big picture" and overall goal into a picture that illustrates individual goals for each employee. Leaders need to answer the question that will be in every worker's mind: What will the changes mean to me and my area of responsibility? Herb Aspbury, Chase Manhattan Corporation's regional executive for Europe, Africa, and the Middle East, told me:

> The leader needs to communicate why we are here—in our business we are here to do specific transactions with specific customers. We need to be clear who those customers are, what products we are trying to sell, and what kind of organization we need to deliver. This needs to be crafted into a vision that is tangible and people can relate to. The second task is to motivate the people to share the vision and deliver. If we have the right product and our people have the wrong attitude, we will fail. Central to the success of the leader is his ability to communicate the vision and mobilize the people.

Managing the context, then, is about conveying what the company holds dear. But that is only a first step.

Following the initial communication, the leader is responsible for presenting a strategy that highlights cultural and performance milestones. This enables employees to assess how they are adapting to the new context. Without this approach and these tools, a company has no chance of winning employees' support for a leader's ambition. In addition, no organization will successfully achieve its ambition unless leaders have a clear and ruthlessly honest view of the new context they are obliged to provide. Skillfully, good leaders will communicate that context via relevant data about the company, especially its shared values, assumptions, and perceptions, as well as information regarding its past and present circumstances, its potential, and its design for reaching that potential.

People's expectations and beliefs are experienced so deeply that they are, in fact, integrated aspects of our identities. These beliefs influence us in every conceivable encounter, whether it is a crucial meeting, a work session, or an informal chat at the water fountain. If the context is not developed and communicated clearly, the obvious result is misunderstanding, which in turn leads to conflicting ideas about who is doing what and why. Chaos and confusion will prevail.

Apple Computer, Inc., of Cupertino, California, offers an excellent example. That Apple was once the "darling" of the computer world, expressed in part by its huge international fan club, did not prevent even its most devoted followers from losing their affection by 1996. Apple's serious problems included its slow-moving efforts to develop a new operating system and the loss of some of its smartest people. Plagued by intraorganization competition, Apple could no longer keep up with the changes the rapidly growing Internet necessitated. Apple became a synonym for discord and upheaval, a widely reported sad fact.

Not until Steven P. Jobs, the founder and original chief executive officer, was appointed to the anomalous position of adviser to the company did its fortunes swing upward. (Later, he was named "interim" chief executive officer, and early this year, Jobs signaled his intention of staying at Apple by dropping the "interim.") Jobs immersed himself in every aspect of Apple, attending meetings on everything from marketing strategy to product review. He restructured the company by narrowing its concentration to four product categories; he repaired Apple's relationship with its programmers, and he repriced workers' stock options to their benefit. Jobs made it clear that he had an ambition for Apple Computer and a strategy for achieving it. He was setting a new context and communicating to employees what he expected them to deliver.

Setting and conveying a context is an enormous challenge that, of course, should not be undertaken without serious consideration. If a leader encounters a fatal flaw in the company or realizes that a fundamental business challenge looms, he or she must, as we discussed in the previous chapter, climb to the balcony. From that vantage point, removed from daily diversions, a leader can view the company in its entirety, gauging the seriousness of the organization's situation. Here is where he or she can begin to develop a new ambition and a new strategy to realize it. From there, leaders can begin to build a business model to accomplish their goals and, hopefully, bring about a brighter future for the company.

Although the path to the new context may be exquisitely clear to leaders, the communication of that plan to the company's workers must be equally clear. Crucial to the ensuing challenge, employees need to understand the company's problems, opportunities, and the context in which this ongoing dilemma arose. That workers comprehend the strategic insights leading to the new context is vital because it will help them to unite behind the leader's initiatives. Without employee support, which demands all of a leader's communication skills, he or she will fail. As Peter Bijur of Texaco wryly observed in a conversation with me, "'I make a speech' doesn't equal 'they understand.'"

Nowhere is a well-communicated shared context more paramount to the company's successful future than in large organizations with hundreds, perhaps thousands, of employees. Whatever techniques a leader employs to create and communicate new ambitions and strategies, the purpose is always the same—to convey a coherent and significant new context for the organization. This applies if the method is the distribution of mission statements that define prospective changes or if the technique is the expression of symbolic gestures enhanced by a touch of showmanship. We can learn from the example of Sir Bryan Nicholson.

In the early 1990s, when I attended a speech of Sir Bryan's in London, he was in his first year as chairman of the British Post Office, a position he has since left. When he took over the post office, everyone, customers and employees alike, agreed that the quality of service was horrendous. During this speech, Sir Bryan indicated that I was working with him to dramatically improve the situation.

Five years later, Sir Bryan had transformed the organization into one of the most customer-responsive post offices in the Western world, and I attribute much of his success to his abilities both to reset his organization's context and, of course, to communicate the direction of that context. He may be the only leader I know who had the organization's mission statement permanently hanging in his office. I sensed that if I awoke Sir Bryan at three o'clock in the morning and asked him to state the vision and mission of the British Post Office, he would do so—not only verbatim, but with passion. "Articulate a clear, simple vision—not 5,000 words," he advises. "Our vision for the Post Office is to be customer-led and market-driven. We will be," he continued, "a profit-making, public service organization providing excellent service achieved through training people properly."

Although anyone might make such a statement, Sir Bryan recognized what was involved in realizing it. As in advertising, the message has to be consistent. "I repeated the message again and again. . . . In every forum, it was the first thing I said," he explained. And Sir Bryan was patient, learning never to tire of repeating the same simple message. Whether the forum called for a one-minute presentation or an hour-long one, his message was always the same. Never had the need for consistency, simplicity, and repetition been greater than in this situation. Because people were bombarded with all sorts of information, it became nearly impossible for them to prioritize it. Even if a message does stand out from the information glut, the listener is unlikely to respond right away.

An experienced leader expects that some people will not have heard the message, no matter how often and in how many different ways it is repeated. Others will remember only the parts they want to hear, which means that the communication may not be understood or acted on as intended, even when a listener thinks otherwise. The key, Sir Bryan believes, is to make sure that "the vision, ambition, or message is not just rational. We needed commitment of the heart, not just the head." He explains:

> This began with my top team and was set against 300,000 rule book–driven employees when we began. We looked immobile. Our message needed to be emotional, not just intellectual. We needed to sing—not just from the same hymnal—[but] singing that same undiluted vision with a passion and vigor the employees in the far rows of the church could hear, understand, and be uplifted by.

Setting a new context requires liberating oneself from the old context, whether that was a set of cumbersome work rules, as was the case at the British Post Office, or a set of outdated beliefs about the working environment.

Peter Bijur encountered the latter not so long ago when Texaco nearly went under. Texaco employees had to abandon the context established in 1980 when crude oil sold for $1.80 a barrel and oil companies made a profit at the wellhead. Then, maximum volume equaled maximum returns. A volume-driven business dependent on multiple distribution channels was enormously different from the climate of the 1990s, when efficiency and cost effectiveness were the critical imperatives. Communicating the changed context—"right-sizing the organization"—in such a way that each individual was helped to understand his or her value within the new environment was central to the turn-around, noted Bijur. Employees were helped to adapt to the changed environment, in which the traditional command-and-control structure gave way to a structure wherein those on the front line were expected to assume more responsibility. Other leaders, both in and out of the oil industry, echoed support for this structural change. Jan Carlzon, for example, spoke of a time when authoritarian corporate leaders ran all aspects of the business in a military command-and-control style. Today, Carlzon wryly perceives that "a command-and-control organization is what you want if you are going to war with your customer." This is well illustrated in the following example.

I was present when Nicholas Temple, chief executive officer of IBM U.K. Ltd., first presented what he called "The IBM Story" to his management board in February 1993. It was what I refer to as a context statement. A year earlier, after the parent company recorded a $5 billion loss, of which $1 billion was attributable to the U.K. operation, Temple introduced a blueprint for change. Since it won only a limited commitment and its implementation was slow, Temple was induced to rethink both the dynamics leading to IBM's business crisis and the nature of its future competition.

On this February day, Temple discussed the values shared by successful entrepreneurs in the computer industry—Steve Jobs, Michael Dell, Bill Gates, and, of course, IBM founder Thomas Watson. Explaining how markets grow organically, he explored the subtleties of managing costs within various stages of business life cycles. In addition, Temple clarified the impossibility of using an outdated command-and-control management style when the goal is to oversee fragmented, highly competitive, organic cells, which, when put together, comprise the industry. In short, he offered his managers a shared historical perspective. Also, he communicated likely future scenarios of customer and competitor dynamics, simultaneously pointing out how old plans, behaviors, and working styles have to change as a precondition of solving IBM's U.K. problems.

Within months of Temple's context-setting statement, IBM U.K. created thirty business units, limited the power of the traditionally strong finance and personnel functions, dismantled headquarters-managed shared services, and reduced the workforce by 30 percent. As a result, instead of the red ink recorded in 1992, IBM U.K. was able to show a solid profit by the end of 1993. An analysis of Temple's approach reveals that he enabled his managers to develop a shared context, which in turn allowed them to understand and appreciate more deeply his blueprint for turning around the U.K. operations. Wisely, he recognized that he had to transform people's perceptions and their contextual perspective before he could expect them to tackle a major challenge that was, by definition, predicated on a process of change.

The capacity to manage context—that is, to communicate a vision in such a way that it will mobilize employees—is central to the leader's ability to bring about adaptive change. According to Sir Bryan Nicholson, it all starts with "an agenda for adaptive change."

Typically, that means six to ten issues or initiatives that must be driven from the top. Together, this collective and coherent agenda is the plan to achieve the vision and create greater customer responsiveness. The agenda needs to be reviewed and refined in the course of the journey. There needs to be a timetable with clear milestones. There must be a sequence of events that, in the end, delivers vision. The leader cannot afford to be diverted by day-to-day operating pressure or quick fixes.

No one understands this better than Gene Fife, former chairman and managing director of Goldman Sachs International Ltd. and now its chief executive officer.

Fife turned Goldman's $200 million European operation into a $1.2 billion business in only five years. Fife reports:

> When we began our European expansion, new hires, senior and junior people alike, felt our guiding principles had been developed by an advertising agency on Madison Avenue. It wasn't until they realized how serious top management was about living these values and having these guiding principles govern our attitudes and behaviors towards customers and colleagues that they began to take hold.

I remember one new senior partner explaining that he had to leave a critical merger discussion because he had a commitment to go to the opera. It was only explained to him once that the customer was paying for the opera ticket. Without customers, we don't need bankers. They are the boss. They pay the light bills. It is our responsibility to deliver quality of service, ethics, and the highest quality of professional work. The guiding principles drive the attributes and behaviors in the organization.

As I listened to Fife express his commitment to the guiding principles of Goldman Sachs, it was clear that employees will either live these values or not fit in. Put bluntly, if someone does not measure up to Goldman's vision and values, he or she will not last long at this leading-edge, customer-responsive, team-oriented bank.

Business history is littered with examples of disasters resulting from leaders' inabilities to articulate guiding principles and set the contexts in which their ambitions can be achieved. In other words, the leader cannot communicate what is real in such a way that managers and employees are inculcated with a coherent set of guiding principles. Few disasters in recent memory can match that of Cendant Corporation, a $14 billion merger of supposed equals, carried out in late 1997. At one level, this debacle is rooted in a massive accounting fraud, which ruined a much publicized merger. At another, its source is the failure of the principal deal makers to develop and articulate a set of guiding values under which the combined company could operate.

Cendant was born of the misbegotten courtship of CUC International, Inc., a Connecticut-based purveyor of shopping-club memberships sold through credit-card companies, and HFS, Inc., a Parsippany, New Jersey, franchiser of several businesses, including real estate brokerages, lodging operations, and car-rental agencies. As *Fortune* magazine described it, even without CUC's subsequently discovered accounting fraud, the combination was "a disaster waiting to happen," because the styles of leadership at HFS and CUC, as well as the companies themselves, were antithetical.

HFS was the brainchild of Henry Silverman, a hard-driving, control-oriented deal maker who, according to *Fortune's* Peter Elkind, paid little, if any, attention to "soft" issues such as culture, corporate values, and employee perceptions. CUC, on the other hand, was led by Walter Forbes, described as dreamy and detached, who viewed himself as a visionary. Forbes was anything but a hands-on leader. It appeared that the only thing Silverman and Forbes shared was an outsized desire to produce greater growth rates and high multiples, so coveted by Wall Street investors. Even if setting the context had been considered, which it almost certainly was not, it is difficult to imagine what that context may have been. In a so-called "merger of equals," in which the culture and leadership models were 180 degrees apart, whose vision and management principles would dictate the combined company's ambition and its path for getting there? Even a cursory look at Silverman's and Forbes's personalities and operating styles suggests that neither could oversee the operations of the other, unless the companies were to change drastically. So regardless of which leader eventually had more authority, his failure seemed inevitable. Discovering fraud merely hastened the all-but-certain disaster.

From its inception, the deal was deeply problematic. For one reason, Forbes and Silverman agreed to a sort of rotating power structure, taking turns running the merged entity. The executive teams, too, were expected to move in and out of power. For another reason, Cendant was structured with two corporate headquarters in different states—New Jersey and Connecticut. Moreover, assuring failure, Forbes's management team continued to run CUC when Silverman was running the overall company. The clarity of hindsight is unnecessary to see that such an arrangement was most likely not workable, and it is surprising that this was not obvious to Silverman and Forbes. Still, this bizarre agreement was just a prelude to the bitter management clash that erupted almost immediately.

Forbes's team found Silverman and his group arrogant and bureaucratic, whereas the HFS contingent characterized the CUC managers as careless, lazy, and inept. Since this was no love match, no honeymoon was in sight, and not much hope that these strange bedfellows could agree on either strategy or cultural and performance milestones. As we have learned, without these, the leaders would not win the minds and hearts of employees. It appeared that Silverman and Forbes neglected to agree on their visions for Cendant, if they were even discussed. It was terrible business practice on everyone's part, worsened by a 1997 earnings restatement indicating a downward spiraling stock price. On both sides, charges and countercharges were rapidly exchanged, culminating in a $47.5 million buyout to remove Forbes from the company. Shareholders brought lawsuits and government investigations ensued. Yet, most revealing of all, Silverman tried to undo the merger by selling off CUC businesses. As 1999 drew to a close, Cendant agreed to pay $2.8 billion to settle a shareholder class action lawsuit alleging widespread accounting fraud. It was the largest settlement ever made in a stockholders' class action, and ended what Henry Silverman understated as "a most unfortunate event."

If Cendant is an extreme example, it nevertheless illustrates what can go wrong when leaders fail to set context. It does not matter if the problem at hand is a major merger or acquisition or the implementation of a seasonal sales plan; employees will not assume responsibility for enacting context without understanding its goals and strategies. They must be able to envision what the company will be at its best, and recognize that the fruition of that vision depends on them. This enables people to determine "what this means to me in my area of responsibility and how it informs my priorities."

As Honeywell's soon-to-retire Larry Bossidy has correctly noted, employees do not like to be treated as if they are children: "They want to be communicated with frequently about how the organization is performing. They want to broaden their skill base. They want to have a chance to own a stake in the companies for which they work." In short, people want to be informed regarding what is going on in their companies, and they want opportunities to contribute. And when good leaders give them that chance, they will invariably deliver. People will have an easier time making a commitment to a leader's vision if they understand not only *what* is expected of them, but *why*. In Larry Bossidy's opinion, employees like to have a clearly defined "goal line, so if they're successful, they have a chance to stop and say, 'Hey, this is a victory.'" Bossidy believes leaders have to set the context, just as Jan Carlzon did for the struggling SAS when, as I discussed in Chapter 4, he focused the entire company on service and presented a convincing rationale that supported his policy of increased responsibilities for frontline workers.

Carlzon calculated that each of SAS's 10 million customers comes into contact with five of the airline's employees for, on

average, fifteen seconds apiece. Though brief, these contacts
are significant, according to Carlzon, and he refers to them as
"moments of truth," because it is here that customers form a
favorable or unfavorable impression of the airline. Since fifteen seconds allows the employee no time to consult a super-
visor, who may need to turn to his or her own boss, it seems
clear that solutions must be determined on the spot. Carlzon's
vision for customer service at SAS required decentralized decisionmaking, meaning that more power was distributed to all
frontline employees. To manage this context, employees were
given center stage. Offered careful training so that they could
accomplish their tasks easily and skillfully, workers' importance and value to the company were acknowledged for the
first time.

John Chambers, chief executive officer of Cisco Systems,
Inc., describing the democratization of decision-making in his
own company, once told Thomas L. Friedman of the *New York
Times:*

> I can only make so many decisions and gather so much information,
> at the pace of today's economy. I want to make the big strategic deci-
> sions, but after that, if I have disseminated the decision-making
> process down to the people who are closest to the action . . . then I
> have a thousand decision-makers working for me, and there is a bet-
> ter chance that we won't miss the market. There is also a better
> chance that they will experiment and find the right answer to some re-
> ally complex problems. Top-down decision making only works where
> the market moves slower or the person at the top is able to keep his or
> her finger on the pulse [of the entire company] all the time, and that
> is very rare these days.

Concentrating on employees is a crucial step for a company
hoping to satisfy customers.

The late Samuel Moore Walton, founder of Wal-Mart Stores, Inc., believed that employees' behavior toward customers reflects how management behaves toward them. In Walton's reasoning, Jan Carlzon applied a variation of the Golden Rule—management should do unto employees as they hope employees would do unto SAS customers. Gene Fife (former chairman and managing director of Goldman Sachs) emphasizes: "The leader must communicate [that] he cares about clients and customers. This must be genuine, not buzzwords. The organization must embrace the fact that the customer runs our business. This attitude must be transmitted to each and every client," which, as Fife knows so well, is how a good leader manages context.

At SAS, Jan Carlzon instituted intensive education for employees to hasten the strategic metamorphosis. As he did so, he made it clear that everyone was expected to assume more responsibility within the new framework. He explains that "anyone who is not given information cannot assume responsibility. But anyone who is given information cannot avoid assuming it. Once they understood our vision, our employees accepted responsibility enthusiastically, which sparked numerous simultaneous and energetic developments in the company."

Famed football coach Bill Parcells echoed Carlzon's thoughts in a speech he gave to employees of Corning, Inc., headquartered in Corning, New York. Invited by Roger Ackerman, the company's chairman and chief executive officer, Parcells described his strategy for victory on the football field. "What winning is in football—and I'll bet it's the same everywhere—is to get everybody on the same page, and then try to get the most out of everybody who's on that field." When employees ask, and eventually must be able to answer for themselves, "What do the changes mean for me?" leaders may struggle to present the necessary information in a clear and understandable form. More-over, and this is important, they should do so with the energy, persuasiveness, and conviction needed to win support for the initiative. Furthermore, "it's easy to slip backwards," notes Nicholas Barber, former chief executive officer of the Ocean Group.

Reminiscent of Bijur's observation—"'I make a speech' does-n't equal 'they understand'"—Barber points out that "you think you are communicating when you are not. You need to build in a way to understand what the audience heard—this is more im-portant than what you said. You need to constantly take stock of how well you are communicating." Not only is it incumbent upon the leader to present her or his vision such that it moti-vates people, but the leader must also confirm with the audi-ence that they interpreted him or her correctly, as she or he intended. It is particularly difficult during the initial stages of communication, especially if the new strategy calls for decen-tralization and, henceforth, employees will be expected to as-sume more responsibility for making decisions.

Can any leader expect to meet and convince every member of a large organization? Of course not. But leaders must be sure that no possible channel of communication has been over-looked. In-house computer networks, closed-circuit television, personal presentations, and small meetings can be used to con-vey a leader's ambition and the plans for achieving it. "In a large organization," Sir Bryan Nicholson said, "you can think you've fixed things when you haven't. You can send 2,000 managers in the wrong direction and two to three years later you find you have missed the mark. You look back and you realize the mes-sage got diluted, the challenge became fragmented, and imple-mentation plans diverged form the original ambition." That is why a leader should never lose an opportunity to communicate his or her message to employees.

Of course, in-person encounters are always more effective and should be used whenever possible. But the chosen method for conveying the message is less critical than a simple, direct presentation. A thorough, sophisticated understanding of corporate strategy at all levels is crucial to the well-being of any organization. Nothing is to be gained by obfuscation and unnecessary complexity.

Carlzon, always a believer in simplicity and clarity, also adopted this approach for his communication outside the company. He insisted on a straightforward presentation of information in both advertising and public relations. For instance, he eschewed meaningless slogans such as, "Give the Swedes the World," and instead opted for practical, catchy, and informative phrases designed to entice travelers: "No need to stand in line" and "As close as you can get to first-class on a coach-class ticket" are examples.

Even showmanship has its place, unless the leader appears superficial or as though he or she has designed the "show" as a distraction from the "real" story. Always, the leader's mission is to introduce the strategy to his or her audience with an enthusiasm and commitment as deep as his or her own. Leaders must do more than just talk to their audiences. They must ignite them.

Equally important, the leader must avoid giving conflicting messages or participating in inconsistent advertising. Through their actions and behaviors as well as their words, leaders define the ambience of their companies. Thus, good leaders do not say one thing to employees and make a conflicting remark to Wall Street analysts. Unconscious, perhaps, to both employee and leader, the latter's conduct and demeanor enormously influence and may determine the feelings and attitudes that permeate the company, from top executives to the rank-and-file.

Still, many leaders accept, without analysis, the privileges of their positions. Elaborately furnished offices, private dining rooms, limousines, and corporate planes are all assumed luxuries for the corporation's top person. When a leader seeks to flatten the company's bureaucracy, however, and redistribute responsibilities for making decisions, he or she is compelled to rethink the meanings of these privileges. Before taking on SAS, Jan Carlzon had served as president of Linjeflyg, Sweden's domestic airline and an SAS affiliate. He had a large, airy office with an open view of the street, with an adjoining personal dining room seating eight. Carlzon decided these privileges conveyed a false sense of his identity and his values and sent the wrong message to workers who ate in the company cafeteria. His changes included turning the private dining room into his office and converting his previous spacious office into a conference room available to all employees. Then, he and his executives began to eat lunch in the company cafeteria. Carlzon intended these modifications to express the sentiment to his workers that "we are all in this together at Linjeflyg." By flattening the chain of command, he created a new context for his workers, in which he emphasized his belief that a leader contributes to a company's image by example.

As I said at the beginning, a leader's attempt to set a new context will be for nothing if the workforce is not fully informed of the company's current circumstances and its future plans. One way of reinforcing the message is to present or issue a context statement. That is what Nick Temple did when he used his version of "The IBM Story" to motivate the company to support his blueprint for change.

Whatever method leaders choose as the vehicle through which to publicize their context statements—oral presentations, pamphlets, small books, or a series of meetings, to name a few options—I strongly suggest that they include an overview of the company's strategic and competitive histories. In other words, describe the company's context as it was before.

The most significant part of the context statement deals with the present business situation and why there is an urgent need for change. Here is where leaders can make compelling arguments for the new context, including discussion of the likely impacts on the company of future economic, technological, and political trends. In addition to educating the workforce regarding management's plans, the statement guides employees in meeting the challenges ahead.

My main point is that the leader must clearly explain his or her new goals and new ambition. Proclamations issued from above with little, if any, explanation have never been successful in motivating workers to do their best.

How Does One Communicate What Is Real?

Here are some ideas.

Craft a Context Statement

To communicate present and future realities to the workforce, leaders should design a context statement, in which they clearly detail the rationale for, and substance of, the new context. This assures that everyone will read from the same page— literally and figuratively. The five elements of the context statement follow:

1. The company's strategic, competitive financial and cultural history, meaning the key milestones in the life of the company.
2. The company's current business situation.

3. The trends—market, customer, economic, technological, and political—that are likely to impact the company's future.
4. A compelling expression of the leader's ambition for the company.
5. What this means for an individual employee in his or her area of responsibility.

The context statement is an important aspect of the real work of a leader.

Manage Your Credibility

"How you manage credibility is a big issue," Jan Timmer, chairman and chief executive officer of Philips Electronics N.V., told me. If you are not credible, people will not follow you; thus, workers will not perform and you will not achieve your ambition. You will lose credibility if you say one thing and do another; always remember that what you say and do are visible to everyone. Leaders cannot fool financial analysts, the stock market, employees, or their customers. You must be honest—always.

Every successful leader knows that credibility and trust cannot be delegated. When a frontline person asks, "When it comes to the crunch, what do you want me to achieve?" the leader needs to offer a simple, clear, and consistent response. If a leader's responses differ depending on who or when one poses the question, that leader loses credibility. Think of a bicycle race—a bicyclist may be keeping pace, but his mistakes are highly visible. Workers and customers want to know what values and points of view the leader represents, especially in difficult financial times, because only then will people invest emotionally in helping to achieve the ambition for the organization.

Manage Expectations

"Reflect on and question what you initially communicated," Timmer advises. "Did you ask too much or promise too much? Did you warn people that setbacks were inevitable? Managing expectations and making sure people understand the task facing them is critical."

Next

Adaptive work always calls for changes within important interorganizational relationships. After all, these internal relationships define a company. Then, a value system appropriate to the new situation, what I refer to in earlier chapters as the company's culture, must be defined. A close examination of current values will most likely reveal the need for modification. Deeply held values and beliefs are not to be discarded, however, without very careful consideration. Values collide; conflicts erupt. Suddenly, the road toward achieving the new ambition just got unnecessarily bumpier. How such situations can be defused is the focus of the next chapter.

6

Clarify Competing Values

IN 1994, RUUD KOEDIJK became chairman of KPMG Netherlands, the Dutch arm of the accounting giant KPMG International. Soon, he realized that the firm was in trouble. It simply wasn't finding the right fields to enter to maintain its growth. Koedijk concluded that the essential structure of the firm was to blame. That structure was a consequence of the company's core value, which had contributed to the entrepreneurial development and growth of KPMG, but now prevented the company from adapting to changing realities in a globalized economy.

The problematical value? Individualism. Although the value of individualism had enabled KPMG to achieve rapid and profitable growth, the successful implementation of the new strategy would require the capacity for collaboration and collective action. The firm was not really a true partnership, but rather a collection of some fiefdoms, each run by one partner, each dedicated to its own profits instead of those of the overall organization. Not that KPMG's entrepreneurial nature was inherently bad. Quite the contrary; it had worked splendidly for decades, fueling extraordinary growth. But situations change, and Koedijk was convinced that without a new structure and a new value system, the firm's potential for growth was nil. He was equally convinced that his partners would never entertain the idea of such a drastic structural overhaul.

Koedijk called a meeting of all 300 partners at which he reviewed the firm's history, current state, and business prospects. He then asked the partners how they would deal with the situation. In the ensuing discussion, he convinced them to focus on articulating a solution for KPMG's problems. Ruud Koedijk is a persuasive man: What the 300 partners agreed to was an effort that would require 60 percent of the time of 100 volunteers over the next four months. The mission was to reinvent KPMG and invent a few billion-dollar businesses.

With twelve senior partners leading the way, the volunteers, who were charged with discovering the future and reinventing KPMG, organized fourteen task forces. Eventually, they found themselves confronting the abyss between the values of the current culture and those required if the firm was to grow. On one side were the values supporting an individualistic, entrepreneurial, authoritarian way of operating. On the other were the values supporting a collective, all-for-one-and-one-for-all interdependent team approach. The investigating partners themselves concluded that the second option was mandatory if the newly generated strategy was to be implemented successfully.

After that, the 100 began to loosen up and enjoy themselves as being self-described "evolutionaries." In one statement, they compared the current firm to a big, clumsy, sleepy hippopotamus that attacked any creature that tried to rouse it. They envisioned the new KPMG as a playful dolphin, eager to learn and happy to swim with the group. They even discarded the firm's formal dress code and took to bopping through the KPMG offices that summer in Bermuda shorts and T-shirts—part of the effort to change the mindset that had long permeated the conservative offices of KPMG.

As the transformation went forward, the team spotted some $600 million (and developed $200 million) worth of new business opportunities. They also led the way to a different set of values that were more in keeping with the firm's new aspirations. In this value system, the most creative minds were rewarded no matter where they were in the organization's hierarchy and were paid the respect formerly reserved for high-ranking managers. Out of this initiative came a distinctly new confidence in the middle ranks: Previously unenthusiastic people grew instantly into spotters of opportunity and seekers of growth, and became adept at identifying new business the world over.

For me, an enthusiastic guide, the revealing moment occurred when I spent a day watching an expert auditor guide a group of senior partners through the complexities of various new opportunities. Those sixty-something men (and they were all men) were very impressed with their teacher, a young woman, still in her twenties, whose authority those now-rapt senior partners would not have acknowledged only a year before.

Adaptive work, as we have seen, requires the leader to change the internal workings of his or her organization. That means changing the relationships between managers and employees, employees and employees, and employees and their jobs. It also means that the values that will characterize these relationships must be determined and, of course, communicated to employees, so that it is very clear to them why these particular behavioral changes are required of them at precisely this time.

In this chapter, I discuss the essential element of adaptive work, showing how one can identify competing values within a company—that is, the values that worked in the past and that will be needed to solve the problems of the future; I provide examples of major corporations that have already done so.

Before we go any further, understand one thing: When I use the word *values,* I intend to denote tangible and practical values that are or will be accepted by all employees as the guiding principles of their behavior at work. I am talking about values pragmatic enough to focus a business on key factors of day-to-day success and concrete enough to guide daily decisionmaking and the resolution of conflicts.

In our personal lives, we all tend to compartmentalize our values. Sometimes we obey them selectively. Sometimes we even deny the essence of a value by following what I call shadow values and what the Buddhists call "near enemies." If the true value is compassion, for example, its near enemy would be pity. When we feel compassion for someone, we identify the sufferer as a person like ourselves, sharing the sorrows of life. Pity puts us on a different, higher plane than the person we feel sorry for.

A similar kind of duality exists in the workplace, and adaptive work succeeds or fails, depending on the choices made between competing values. The choices are not simple because it is not as though one choice is morally right and the other is morally wrong. In the case of KPMG, the competing values were individualism and teamwork. Other companies have varying degrees of one or the other. Since neither value is inherently bad or good, the question becomes which style is better suited to address the task at hand. Deeply held values can block one's ability to find the right answer. The silo mentality may be so deeply established and supported by the levers of control that operate within an organization (for example, compensation structure, organization structure, and so forth) that leaders cannot imagine any other way of conducting business or defining the work that people in the organization do.

Values have to be so profound that they touch the hearts and minds of everyone in the organization. Ideally, in adaptive work, each person finds a way to relate the organization's new ambition to his or her own aspirations and, at some point, identify with the new values. Of course, organizations need energized, committed leaders and employees. If work is going to have any meaning for them, they must find a personal connection to the organization's values, or try to change the values so that they can accept them.

It used to be easier. In times past, managers and employees had a social contract, in which they mutually agreed on a system of prioritized values and how both parties would live by those values. Employees agreed to provide an honest day's labor in return for decent wages and decent working conditions. Managers were tough but fair, and committed to "their" people. Employees spent their entire careers with a single company, and were committed to that company.

Today, the social contract is virtually nonexistent. The layoffs of the last decade outmoded such contracts. Moreover, the widespread use of temporary employees who perform the same jobs as full-time employees, but receive much less pay and no benefits, have made the contracts obsolete. Neither side of the great corporate divide offers loyalty and commitments lightly. Most companies, focusing on the short-term market value of their stock, view workers as units of production and treat them accordingly. If you do not measure up, you lose your job. In the culture of Silicon Valley, people switch jobs frequently and may be considered "odd" for staying with the same company for a long period of time, not to mention the dot.com world, where working for three companies in three years is a badge of honor.

The short-term approach, with its element of discipline, can produce results, but usually the results are also short term. For companies to successfully meet and conquer the challenges of today's business environment, they have to learn to adapt, and the traditional tough-minded approach is not designed for change. Its values are not calculated to make workers feel committed to collective action in a new direction.

To be sure, the leaders of companies who ruled in the old style can point to an organization's collection of values, usually set down in elaborate script and placed in a gold frame. These are values invented and polished by human resources and advertising people, and eventually signed without much consideration from the chief executive.

In my work, I have often asked clients to spell out their companies' real values, the core principles that guide behavior. For example, the real values of the London police force was expressed to me as this: "Figure out what the boss wants to happen, and then make it happen"—not words one is likely to see displayed on the wall or printed in the employees' handbook.

Frequently, my clients are unable to remember or recite their values. Whatever the stated values are, they are sometimes worthless. The workers care about them as much as the chief executive, which is to say not at all. The true values of the organization, the set of beliefs and ideals that motivate the workers from day to day, are very different.

In recent years, there have been signs that a new kind of social contract may be in its infancy. Corporate leaders are beginning to understand that workers' loyalty to one another as well as to their companies determines the level of effectiveness of collective action and ultimately the company's performance. That is particularly true for those who are phasing out a command-and-control organizational structure to implement a system featuring greater employee responsibility.

Typically, in a command-and-control organization, the leader, who is responsible for all of the problem solving, views employees as nothing more than those who implement strategy. The central values of the company culture are obedience and conformity. The leader tells employees what to do and the cultural environment, enforced by managers, shows them how to do it. In such a company, people dress and act alike. Those who do not conform are noticed, not only because they have made a mistake or broken a rule, but because they have betrayed a company value. Certainly, differences are not valued.

Suppose, all of a sudden, the leader recognizes that the financials are not what they should be, and prospects are looking dire. His or her board convinces him or her to hire a consultant, who insists that command-and-control management is outmoded and inefficient. The consultant says it is time to establish new relationships with employees, in which workers should be given more freedom to make decisions, to tap their own expertise and ideas, and given the training and tools to do so. The leader, who attempts to operate in new terrain, says to employees: "We are putting in all these wonderful new information systems, and it is up to you to find the great opportunities that will lift your company to new heights. When problems arise, I'm always ready to listen and contribute, but the decisions are yours. With the help of these systems, we believe that your collective wisdom will find the right answers. We are counting on you."

The employees, of course, are ill prepared for such a role. They have been living in a different land under a different set of rules. The relationships among and between themselves and the leadership team were carved in stone decades earlier when the company was founded. Their definitions of trust, respect, and commitment have become encrypted with negative values.

When a problem or an opportunity rises under the new management system, the results are predictable. Company performance is handicapped by remnants from the command-and-control system of values. How can employees succeed as teammates for the common cause when distrust lingers? How can there be real respect when second-guessing remains the order of the day?

As a result, the foundation of the solution collapses. Employees will not make commitments to each other, and without commitment, there can be no serious pledge to collective action. Lacking an agreement to work as a team, employees are not motivated to develop the fresh ideas they so desperately need to improve performance.

If a leader is contemplating a shift from the top-down management model, a switch from an individualistic, entrepreneurial culture to a collective, team-based mode of operating, or to any kind of initiative that will require renovation in his or her style of responding to problems, prepare for a major cultural change. Current values will have to be closely examined in light of the new responsibilities people will be expected to take on. Inevitably, they will have to be modified or cast off in favor of a set of values more appropriate to the tasks at hand.

When I explain my ideas about competing values and the importance of recognizing them as part of adaptive work to a client organization, I generally start by interviewing anywhere from 30 to 100 people occupying a wide range of jobs and titles. I ask them to tell me the values that underpin the company. Usually, their answers sound like this: "Customers are our first priority and we listen to them." "We believe in teamwork." "We solicit and respect the views of our colleagues." Then I ask them how well the company really does at living up to those values, and those answers sound like this: "Our teamwork is pretty good, but I guess we're not exactly off the charts." Or, "We probably treat customers better than we used to, but it's still not great."

Once a company starts to examine itself from this perspective, bringing to light the discrepancies between stated values and the way the company actually operates, the lack of a shared value system takes on weight. The company's leaders begin to recognize what lies at the root of their performance problems.

You can not sit at the elbow of every employee every minute, monitoring and guiding his or her decisions and behavior. You have to assume that their fondness for a paycheck will keep them working hard and well. Moreover, you have to rely on their acceptance, whether conscious or unconscious, of a set of shared values that comes with the corporate territory. If the values are not what they need to be to attain the desired collective action or if the values are right but the commitment to them is lacking, the company will not be able to pursue adaptive work successfully. At least, to my knowledge, it has never happened.

After I interview client companies on the subject of their stated values, I ask them if there are any competing values at work in their organizations. Finally, the floodgates open. "We are constantly being second-guessed," they say. Or, "We get mixed signals from top management." Or, "People make mistakes and won't take responsibility for them."

I remember asking a senior executive of an oil company what competing values existed in his firm. The question excited him. "Mistrust!" he shouted. "It's everywhere." He strode to his door and threw it open. "Can't you smell it?" he asked. "You can cut it with a knife." I asked how I could recognize it. "Everybody is second-guessing everybody," he said. "Nobody shares information. Everybody has his head down and operates according to his own agenda."

After we complete this question-and-answer process, the leaders of most companies are ready to talk about competing values and how to reconcile them. They must think seriously about the attitudes their workers hold toward the company, such as: What kinds of behaviors are understood to be acceptable? How much of a commitment do employees have to their colleagues and the company as a whole? In other words, how do the company's current values compare with the optimal values necessary to encourage the kind of teamwork adaptive work demands?

Apart from the specific, tangible values that will be dictated by the particular problem, my research shows that there are three primary adaptive values that must exist at the heart of any corporate culture that is aiming to achieve effective collective action. Each adaptive value, of course, has a corresponding competing value. They are trust versus mistrust; respect versus disrespect; commitment versus apathy. Unlike my description of subordinate competing values as neither good nor bad, but simply inappropriate for the task at hand, the flip sides of these core values are bad. They create a negative atmosphere that makes it impossible for a company to achieve a leader's ambition.

Before we get into a description of each competing value, I want to introduce two companies whose cultures have been painstakingly designed to nurture collective action in pursuit of adaptive change and high performance. They will provide chapter and verse for the discussion of the three primary values and their opposites.

The first is the Albert Einstein Healthcare Network, a Philadelphia-based health care conglomerate encompassing primary-care physicians, hospitals, home care, nursing homes, rehabilitation centers, and educational programs. Some years ago, worried that his organization lacked the flexibility it needed to compete in a rapidly changing industry, Martin Goldsmith, chief executive officer, set Albert Einstein on a new path. In the past, the organization had been dedicated to maintaining its status as one of the best hospital systems in its area, judged by the percentage of its beds that were filled at any given time. Because the changing face of health care made it harder and harder to fill beds, Goldsmith insisted that the network should be judged by the improved health of its individual patients. Workers would be expected to do whatever was necessary to meet the new goal, even if it involved devising expensive new solutions.

Goldsmith knew that his strategy could not be achieved within the organization's existing paternalistic culture. He set out to change both the culture and the values that underlay that culture—values that designated executives as supreme authority figures, for instance, to the detriment of the many other health care professionals who make up the hospital team. It was not an easy task. Values that are accepted as guiding principles are, by definition, deeply held and not easily changed. The process took about seven years. But Albert Einstein emerged stronger than ever.

The second example is Whole Foods Market, Inc., the largest natural-foods grocer in the United States. Starting with a tiny market in Austin, Texas, in 1980, Whole Foods has grown to a network of forty-three upscale, environmentally-oriented stores in ten states, with revenues of $500 million a year. It represents what *Fast Company* calls "one of the business world's most radical experiments in democratic capitalism."

The employees at every Whole Foods market are divided into ten teams—produce, grocery, nutrition, bakery, and the like. Each team has its designated leader and meets at least once a month after work. Each store as a whole meets once a month, too. Workers are expected to express their concerns, gripes, and suggestions. The company regularly provides its workers with statistics on everything from sales and profitability to service and quality scores for every store and every team throughout the company. Bonuses and promotions depend in part upon how teams perform in comparison with their counterparts elsewhere.

"We don't have lots of rules handed down from Austin," John Mackey, cofounder, chairman, and chief executive officer, has said. "We have lots of self-examination going on. Peer pressure substitutes for bureaucracy." That means Whole Foods employees are expected to live the values of teamwork without being pressed from on high.

We will revisit Einstein and Whole Foods as we move on to examine the three sets of competing values: trust versus mistrust, respect versus disrespect, and commitment versus apathy.

Trust Versus Mistrust

By way of a reminder, I am not talking about a feeling of trust we associate, in general, with social contracts: For example, that one trusts his neighbor on the assembly line not to steal one's wallet. I am talking about a specific feeling of trust that you experience for your leader and coworkers, which allows you to work together cooperatively, sharing information for the purpose of meeting a goal or accomplishing a project. In this context, people feel their opinions are listened to and taken seriously. One trusts them because one knows they will do their part of the job to the best of their abilities and because they will not arbitrarily fire or let you down if a problem arises. Put another way, the team wants to get the job done and receive collective credit. At the Albert Einstein Healthcare Network, the adaptive work started with the leadership cadres. It took two years before Goldsmith, the chief executive, felt ready to move it down into the company ranks.

At meetings attended by Goldsmith and his executives, a list of values was drawn up and worked through. Two kinds of trust were listed. One was the trust they hoped to inspire in patients and suppliers: "We promote trust through our honest transactions." The other was trust within the institution itself, which was captured in the value, "We rely on each other."

First, teams of executives, and later, teams of employees, met to determine how the various values should be implemented. At these sessions, Goldsmith insisted on frankness and openness.

He encouraged debate about competing values and about how desired values might become manifest in individual behaviors. During one meeting, he was informed that he lacked a team-oriented approach. Goldsmith's willingness to accept correction went a long way toward building trust.

Trust was also nurtured at meetings of interdisciplinary teams, where employees from different parts of the organization met for the first time. More than anything else, though, Goldsmith's basic approach to the adaptive work built trust between leaders and workers. His plan was not popular with his employees. Half of them had fifteen or more years of service and were comfortable in the old culture. They were not inclined to welcome change or anything that implied risk.

The chief executive might simply have steamrolled his plan through. Instead, he proposed the adaptive initiative to all of his workers and promoted understanding by encouraging dialogue. He set up elaborate systems and courses to assist employees in preparing themselves for a whole new way of working. He moved slowly, carefully, giving everyone time to get used to the changes and adapt to them. That approach made it much easier to trust the boss—and his policies.

At Whole Foods Market, where the entire operation is based on the team structure, high levels of trust within the team are mandatory. One way the company builds that trust is to give each team the final say over who will be hired to join that team. The store manager proposes candidates for a team, who are then given a thirty-day trial. After that, they must be approved by a two-thirds vote of their teammates before they can be hired. That power builds coherence, team pride, and great mutual trust.

Salary and bonus figures are among the numbers the company shares with workers. By doing so, the company eliminates an area of secrecy that has long bred mistrust among workers everywhere. It also demonstrates supreme confidence in its workers' ability to handle this delicate information in a mature fashion. And they do. Once they get accustomed to the open-salary idea, most employees pay little attention to others' incomes.

Respect Versus Disrespect

Respect is the second core adaptive value. Again, I am not referring to the respect one feels for a friend or colleague's religious beliefs, or the way she cares for her family, or her success in kicking a cigarette habit. Rather, it is the respect you feel for the ability of the next person on the line or the other members of your team to add value to the common task, to contribute to team performance.

Respect heads the list of values at Albert Einstein, and it is expressed this way: "We show respect for the work and ideas of others." It is a lived, meaning an enacted, concept in that executives exhibit new respect for peers and subordinates. More likely to pick up the phone or walk down the hall instead of sending a memo, they consult with each other more often before making decisions. Workers have discovered new respect for the talents and wisdom of their colleagues, which has led to an enhanced process of sharing ideas and suggestions, which can only benefit patient care.

At Whole Foods, management indicates its respect for workers in the way it shares store, team, and individual progress measures. "In most companies, management controls information and therefore controls people," Mackey told *Fast Company.* "By sharing information, we stay aligned to the vision of shared fate." In other words, his no-secrets philosophy reflects a culture that values and nurtures mutual respect and responsibility.

One method that Whole Foods uses to motivate its employees and reinforce its culture of respect is a system of inspections conducted by workers from other stores as well as by headquarters officials and regional leaders. Stores are rated on 300 measures, and the results are posted in every store in the chain. Team leaders and store managers are expected to note which stores score highest and seek advice on best practices. Employees' salaries, bonuses, and careers are linked to their team's score on these inspections. The team score depends in turn on the abilities of the team members to jointly achieve their goals—an effort that is strengthened by mutual feelings of trust and respect.

Commitment Versus Apathy

The third of the primary adaptive values, commitment, develops from the first two. When one trusts and respects the people with whom they work, one is more willing to commit to them in pursuit of a common goal. One of the great myths of management is that people commit themselves to a strategy. In fact, people commit to each other, not to a strategy. Building commitment is the real work of a leader.

I am sure you have attended a meeting that ends with the leader asking each participant, one by one, "Are you committed?" Of course, everyone says yes. The answer is as meaningless as the question is misguided. In such a situation, is it likely that anyone will say, "Well, as a matter of fact, J. B., I'm not committed"? Real commitment is demonstrated by behavior and performance. It is visible in each and every meeting, presentation, and report.

Conversely, time and again I have observed senior executives point out problems to other executives in a way that I describe as "from the dock." They are extremely skilled at detailing problems in areas where they themselves bear no responsibility, or for which the top team is collectively responsible. They see themselves neither as part of the problem nor as part of the team. The dock offers a different perspective from that of the boat, where the team is working together to solve problems in a strong wind or raging currents when the motor has conked out. From the dock, there is an easy escape directly back to shore.

Individual executives with private or personal agendas use this exit route all the time, even though this attitude is always highly visible to the executive team. Most of the time it is visible to the next two tiers of management, as well. When people work as a team, seek the opinions of others, and engage in open dialogue in the process of reaching a decision, they are expressing their commitments to one another, to the work at hand, and to the company's larger ambition. This is what adaptive work does. In technical work, where solutions are more clear-cut (remember the example of the surgeon's scalpel), the priorities and values are quite different.

At Albert Einstein, the emphasis on commitment pervades the company's list of values: "We are loyal to our organization and our values." "We rely on each other." "By giving our support and cooperation, we make each other stronger." Martin Goldsmith revealed himself as a true leader when he modeled the commitment that he was requiring of everyone else. In his adaptive effort, he reached out to employees on every level, listened to their comments and complaints, and treated them as colleagues to whom he had committed himself and whose enthusiastic support he deeply desired.

Goldsmith might have made it easier for himself if he had simply fired workers who were slow or unwilling to join the early stages of the adaptive work. He insisted, however, upon giving everyone leeway, and he arranged classes and advisory processes to smooth the transition. When some of his senior people continued to oppose the transformation and refused to work as part of a team by making a commitment to their colleagues and the new context, Goldsmith did not hesitate to dismiss them. No adaptive work can succeed, he realized, without the commitment of senior management. Ralph Larsen, of Johnson & Johnson, is known among his executive team as someone who will bend over backward to work on an adaptive solution until everyone is comfortable with it. Still, even he admits that "there's only so much time that I put into that effort before I change the people."

At Whole Foods, failure to commit to the team is the cardinal sin. Some years ago, Aimee Morgida, a manager of a company market in Cambridge, Massachusetts, rejected a candidate for a team position because three of his team members criticized him for standing around with his hands in his pockets, leaning against the counter, in front of customers. Team members, who are committed to each other and to the store's values, were dismayed by the candidate's apathy and his cavalier attitude toward customers. When he defended himself by saying he didn't realize he had committed such a serious offense, Morgida said that his defense only reinforced her determination to dismiss him. He had failed to absorb the values of his team.

These examples illustrate how commitment is expected and necessary in adaptive work in order to achieve and maintain collective action. Apathetic workers or managers can derail a transformation in no time.

How Does One Clarify Competing Values?

What are the values a company must embrace to accomplish adaptive work? This illustration, in which Hewlett-Packard is thinking about the values it will adopt in order to determine its strategy on an important issue, points out that "values," in the sense that I am discussing them, have no intrinsic worth, but, instead, are contingent upon a company's specific needs at a particular time.

Although Johnson & Johnson and Hewlett-Packard are what Lew Platt tentatively calls "conglomerates," neither has businesses within its company that run with the same independence as those within General Electric. In my 1997 interview with Platt, he told me that HP was struggling to decide upon its strategy regarding intraorganizational businesses. He poses the question this way: "Do we want to continue to go through the agony of trying to get cross business organizations and cross business programs working well; or, do we simply say we are going to forgo those opportunities" and encourage people to continue achieving in their separate areas?

Comparing styles of leadership, Platt told me that "Jack Welch [GE's chairman and chief executive officer] doesn't spend a minute trying to get his appliance people working with his jet engine people. Not a minute. . . . [Yet, HP's] businesses are more closely related than his," which affords HP opportunities for a move toward independent, separate businesses while, at the same time, suggests advantages for a move toward more collaboration across specialty areas. How can one distinguish these values from the countervalues that inhibit or prevent the establishment of a new context? I end this chapter with a fictional exchange between two kinds of leaders—one whose company is an entrepreneurial start-up and the other who heads up a big company spin-off. The different values they express apply to different kinds of situations. I offer it as a tool for spotting the competing values in your organization.

- *Value:* "I expect my people to take the initiative in solving problems and seizing opportunities. I want them to grab the ball and run with it."

- *Countervalue:* "Independence is important, of course, but we are responsible to our stakeholders. We must have some real control, some checkpoints along the way to prevent embarrassing missteps."
- *Value:* "I want to create confidence in the ranks. Confidence leads to risk taking, which leads to success."
- *Countervalue:* "We want to avoid failure. We closely monitor performance and punish failure."
- *Value:* "I respect my employees' innovative ideas. Above all, we want to be agile and quick in responding to the market. Experiment, adapt, experiment again—that's the key to getting out ahead of the pack."
- *Countervalue:* "First, show me the facts. We'll analyze them before we move. We may lose some speed, but we have to be thorough. After all, we have a corporate name and reputation to worry about."
- *Value:* "Getting to the market first is what we're all about."
- *Countervalue:* "We've got so much weight and power behind us that we must take our time. When we decide to get rolling, nobody can stop us."
- *Value:* "We know that upstarts just like us are out there waiting to eat our lunch. We're edgy. We're paranoid. We're ready to jump when we see an opening."
- *Countervalue:* "Relax. Why look for trouble? The XYZ Corporation's way of doing things has worked well for a long time. Prudence is the company's byword when it comes to making major investments, and we don't want to rock the boat."
- *Value:* "I encourage my employees to speak their minds. If someone thinks we're doing something wrong, I want to hear about it. If someone has a beef, I say put it on the table so we can hash it out."

- *Countervalue:* "Everyone is entitled to his or her opinions, of course. But it's better for the company overall if we keep conflict to a minimum. Anyway, how likely is it that one person will spot a valid concern that hasn't already been considered by our seasoned team of executive decisionmakers?"
- *Value:* "We're a company of entrepreneurs, up and down the ladder. Entrepreneurs make the key decisions."
- *Countervalue:* "Sure, I applaud entrepreneurial workers, but they have to get approval from senior executives and operate within the system. Teamwork is what it's all about."

I cede the final word on values to Dee Ward Hock, founder and chief executive officer emeritus of Visa International: "An organization's success has enormously more to do with clarity of a shared purpose, common principles, and strength of belief in them than to assets, expertise, operating ability, or management competence."

Next

The heart of adaptive work beats in the chests of individual employees. Their acceptance of a new set of values makes the solution possible. In the next chapters, I discuss techniques that can be applied to achieve this acceptance. In the next chapter, I show how you can nurture values and I offer a number of detailed case histories of companies that have pursued adaptive work on the way toward a successful transformation.

7

Support Changes in Values

LET ME INTRODUCE YOU to a leader named Matt. You have never met him, but I am sure you will recognize his type.

An executive vice president with a major corporation, Matt is responsible for 30 percent of the revenue of a business unit that generates 40 percent of the company's profits. He is charming, even charismatic, and a gifted speaker. He is recognized as the company's best negotiator, and will always support his line managers by helping them close important deals. He is the number one salesperson in a sales-driven organization, working fifteen-hour days. People who deliver for Matt get promoted, and he takes care of their careers. If the chief executive wants something done, he gives the task to Matt, because Matt is the best.

At the same time, many employees within the organization express deep-seated concerns regarding Matt's personal values. Everyone knows he offers different interpretations of the same event to different people. People who cross him can expect retribution. Those who disagree can expect to have their motives openly questioned. He often turns his formidable negotiating skills toward sabotaging colleagues' decisions that get in the way of his own agenda. He has no interest in teamwork—personal power is his single-minded goal, because Matt is the worst.

In recent years, changes in its industry have placed the company's earnings under severe pressure. The board of directors and chief executive officer know that the organization must adapt to new conditions. Matt's skills seem to be essential in moving the company beyond its near-term crisis. His negative values, however, present a roadblock to defining and nurturing the values the company must embrace if it is to improve performance in the long term.

Although I have changed the details of Matt's company and career, he is nonetheless real: I have encountered a few people like him during my years of advising companies. They sometimes occupy leadership roles in leading organizations, and they present a major dilemma for companies. Norman Sanson, managing director at McKinsey & Company, Inc., experienced just such a real-life predicament with a brilliant director who was much sought after by clients, but despised by colleagues.

Sanson reports that this particular fellow lacked concern for people. He abused his team by setting unrealistically high expectations and then demanding that they meet them. He thought nothing of making a team work through a weekend to deliver work to a client ahead of schedule. He took advantage of his team, rather than developing it. Sanson saw immediately that, brilliant or not, this consultant's behavior was incompatible at the firm. He needed to "learn the primacy of people over intellectual horsepower," Sanson told me, adding:

> I was prepared to work with him and made it clear I would do everything I could do to help.

[The director] learned that being very smart and tough on people was no longer sufficient. The days of people not changing roles or companies are gone forever. The idea that talented people will build a career with an organization—ours or elsewhere—is also gone. Leaders can no longer expect unswerving loyalty; they need to adapt to new people and find ways to keep them.

That means it is critical for each manager to learn to live by the values regarding relationships and people. If we fail to do this, we will not keep the best. They will have the other professional lifestyle choices.

This is easier said than done. We need to relearn the importance of living by our principles.

When faced with the necessity of solving life-threatening problems, organizations must perform the adaptive work needed to change direction.

As I noted in the previous chapter, that process demands an examination of the company's current values and clarification of the values needed to achieve the leader's ambition. Employees at odds with the task at hand must be dismissed, whereas those that further the goal must be encouraged throughout the organization. This is the real work of a leader.

In this chapter, I show how successful leaders have initiated changes in values that are vital to their company's excellence. I also point out ways in which they stand behind changes in the face of opposition and appeals to return to old ways.

All the successful examples share at least one crucial component: a leader who actually lives by the values he or she preaches. Leaders like Matt are a clear and present danger to any solution that requires adaptive work. In a conversation with me, Jan Carlzon of SAS put it this way: "Leaders manage values. Leadership is not down to details. The leader must have a view on the culture required to deliver business results and provide people with an opportunity for meaning in work. You walk the talk and you are credible. If you don't, you're not credible and everyone knows it."

Echoing Carlzon's message, Lord David Sainsbury, chairman of J. Sainsbury plc, asserts that:

When it comes to the crunch, there is no sense having a vision and then letting a shoddy product out the door and saying, "we'll fix it next time." That's a very strong message, but don't have the illusion you can have it both ways. If you want commitment and trust within the fabric of the organization, you had better live the ideal you represent. You had better underpin that through rewards and commitment to your people. You lead by what you do. Let me tell you a story about my cousin John [Sir John Sainsbury, recently retired chairman of the company]. One Monday, John came back from holiday to find there was a poor selection of vegetables [in the Sainsbury shops]. The buyers explained that vegetables are picked on Saturday, packed on Sunday, and transported on Monday and Tuesday. Fresh vegetables are available on Wednesday. It was all very logical.

John, however, was furious. He got all the buyers together and instructed the suppliers to meet the same standards of quality every day of the week. The suppliers thought it was a negotiating ploy. The cost, including overtime, was 50 percent higher. There were difficult problems to be solved, but accepting an uneven quality of service to Sainsbury's customers was not one of the options.

Today, Sainsbury's customers are offered the full range of quality products every day of the week.

Sir Colin Marshall is another corporate leader who truly embodies the ideals he represents. When he became chairman and chief executive officer of British Airways in 1982, the government-owned company was a lackluster performer that required subsidies. Within a decade, spurred by a dramatic transformation of its values and culture, the company tripled revenues and raised operating earnings from a deficit of $92 million to a profit of $310 million.

When Sir Colin first arrived at British Airways (BA), he discovered that the company was a collection of fiefdoms, with each department an entity unto itself. People in one department made decisions with little regard for those in others. Each maintained tight control over his or her members and always vied for more power within the larger organization. He found that this silo mindset severely hampered the company's capacity for adapting to new strategic problems. Marketing did not work well with sales; baggage handling was a separate operation with its own goals and objectives; worst of all, customers were often treated as a nuisance.

BA employees had long since become accustomed to this way of conducting business. They preferred working separately, where they had established relationships and were certain of each other's loyalties; they resisted assignments to crossfunctional teams, where conflict and internal competition prevailed, and did poorly if forced to participate. In fact, crossfunctional teams were usually ineffective, because each team member was more interested in representing his or her silo than in collaborating.

Suffering the impediments of this attitude, focused solely on operations, the airplane-flying public turned the acronymic joke, BA stands for "bloody awful," into a serious statement about performance. Sir Colin identified the company's primary challenge, to break through the walls of the silos and build a culture of cooperation, and he uncovered the competing values within the organization. Next he had to clarify the kinds of behaviors that he thought would bring about success in the company. His plan also required adaptive work—that is, he had to put his aides and the workforce in general to work on changing the offending values. One thing Sir Colin did not do was to provide an instant solution. Employees with a particular problem would have to make adaptations.

It soon became evident to Sir Colin that the competing values of trust and mistrust were the foremost problems within the company's culture. Clearly, trust had to be established and reinforced, but the task was daunting. Surveys administered to the airline's employees showed that from a choice of twenty-five behaviors and attitudes critical to the operating of the company, the one identified as most important was trust. Significantly, employees listed trust as the value that was given the most "lip service." Mistrust was rampant, and subordinates acted only on instructions from senior people—that is, they didn't act independently. Functional barriers were well established. The term "smokestacks" was adopted to describe the process whereby each decision had to be approved by the top tier of a function. People feared hostility from their managers, which made them understandably reluctant to own up to problems.

Sir Colin believed that mistrust had to be banished from his company. As he told his employees:

> Trust provides "the glue" which holds people and organizations together. Without trust, staff become merely groups of individuals operating in an uncoordinated way. People need to feel [that] they will be supported when they act in a reasonable manner, [and] that their needs will be fairly considered. Only then will they take constructive risks. The manager must demonstrate trust and a sense of concern for the well-being of others.

Sir Colin's successful overhaul of British Airlines can be attributed in large part to his ability to key in to an important, but intangible issue—that of trust, to represent it so that people feel as if they can touch and see it, and then convey its significance to the entire organization.

When he arrived, Sir Colin sensed the workers' pessimism, but he perceived that beneath low morale, employees were loyal to the company and felt a genuine desire to see it succeed. Clearly, they wanted to work for a successful company, but they were stuck. Sir Colin recognized their need for confidence to do what needed to be done. He concentrated on developing a trusting environment in which colleagues could work comfortably in crossfunctional teams to solve problems and thus improve performance for the customer as well as the bottom line. The real measure of a culture change is a trusting customer and a trusting employee. If customers trust a company, they will come back to do business. Likewise, if employees trust each other, they can work together. Lacking trust, employees will not work together and the customer will forget them.

Sir Colin launched a number of initiatives to convey the desired values and the purpose of the organization. One of the most important, "Managing People First," is a learning program for 1,200 managers across all functions from around the world that demonstrates links between strategic aims of the company and attitudes and behaviors of the workforce, including managers.

The program emphasized how mistrust and its accompanying fear can emotionally paralyze people. In addition, the program pointed out that what managers actually did and how they behaved was more important than their verbal skills. Managers would have to model the new values they were learning if they wanted their teams to adopt them. This could lead to greater effectiveness in groups or teams. In the end, groups or teams that function as a unit, not individuals, create miracles for customers and colleagues.

Participants in the program received feedback from subordinates and team members on twenty specific attitudes and behaviors that were identified as areas that critically required improvement such as customer responsiveness, trust, and teamwork. The feedback was discussed in small working groups, in which individuals were urged to develop and discuss personal action plans for improving areas of weakness and living in accordance with the values in his or her area of responsibility. For example, a manager might receive feedback that his behavior was in the bottom 20 percent of managers in the areas of integrity and trust. His weaknesses included an overly defensive response when others disagreed with him and failure to ensure a frank and open exchange at work-group meetings. The findings were discussed with his manager. On a ten-point scale, he received only a five on "ensuring a frank and open exchange in meetings." Then his manager might suggest that they discuss unacceptable results and assess possibilities of improvement, without which the manager would be dismissed.

During the transformation of British Airways, no one lived in accordance with the company's values more than Sir Colin Marshall. Each Friday for two years he met with groups of twenty-five managers, all of whom were concluding a one-week program on the need to internalize specific values to make BA more competitive and profitable. Week after week he listened patiently to the practical, down-to-earth questions and concerns of managers. Often the questions pointed out the gap between managers' words and actions. Concerns included issues of safety, the lack of sufficient resources on particular flights, or conflicts across departments. Each question or comment represented a test for Sir Colin. Would he respond with the platitudes and evasions of the past, or with the concerned interest and straight talk he had promised as part of the campaign to develop and nurture trust? In the weekly meetings, he answered consistently according to the values he was promoting. He took notes on index cards, which made people feel that he was genuinely interested. When he returned to his office, he immediately acted to correct mistakes and right wrongs.

People saw results quickly. It became clear that Sir Colin was not going to waiver in his commitment to new values and the new culture. Indeed, he could be trusted. His aides took note and followed his lead. Once the experience of trust felt genuine, people within the organization were encouraged to take risks and fix things in their areas of responsibility. Getting people to simultaneously become accountable at all levels turned out to be a central factor in the turnaround of BA.

Why, then, are so many companies incapable of achieving that kind of success? One reason is that negative values permeate managerial ranks. In his classic book on leadership, John Gardner talks about an exemplar of negative values—the turf defender. Here is how he describes an employee of a large government agency in the 1940s:

> Too timid to lead, too vain to follow, his game was turf defense. He was a master of the hidden move and the small betrayal. He understood with a surgeon's precision the vulnerabilities of his colleagues, and he masked calculated unresponsiveness in a thousand innocent guises. As a young observer eager to understand bureaucracy, I found him an open [textbook].

The turf defender's mistrust, and the mistrust he or she sows among colleagues, saps energy and enthusiasm from any organization. As Henry Ford told Gardner, "I try to remind them that the enemy is not the guy across the hall. It's the guy out there selling Chevys."

Elsemo Piol, former vice chairman and chief executive officer of Olivetti Systems & Networks srl, made the same point to me a number of years ago when I asked him who his toughest competition was. After a long pause, he responded, "my service department."

Once a leader recognizes the intimate connection between values and performance, the next question tends to be: "How do we make values tangible and translate them into action?" At Goldman Sachs, neither of its two major conflicting values—individuality and teamwork—is inherently negative, but each represents an ongoing problem. This is how Gene Fife framed it for me:

> Goldman Sachs is filled with creative artists. That's our corporate edge. This individuality can lead to constant tension. The positive is reinforced by the way you have to behave with the team and with the client.
>
> Constant feedback to the individual and compensation related to teamwork [are] critical. Our values or guiding principles, among other things, reinforce teamwork—we are not interested in the "star system" here at Goldman Sachs. That said, internal competition is fierce. There is only a small chance of making partner. This can lead to a "get-out-of-the-way-and-let-me-in-there" mentality. They tell the boss, "No problem, we'll have it done tomorrow," and nearly kill the people working for them in order to deliver on time.
>
> These things must be kept in check. Unmanaged and unled, these forces can be destructive. Everything else gets squeezed out.

How Does One Support Changes in Values?

For adaptive change to be successful, new values must be made explicit and their importance constantly reinforced. Conflicting values cannot be allowed to take precedence. One method used by the leaders of Goldman Sachs is to draw up a list of fourteen business principles, or values. I recommend designing such lists to all my clients. Of course, the effort devoted to creating it and the energy expended on getting managers and the workforce to embrace it determines the worth of any such list. Recall from Chapter 6 that Albert Einstein Medical Center had great success when the executive committee created a comparable list as part of its adaptive work. Goldman Sachs met both requirements fully. Their business principles were carefully crafted with substantial input from around the company, and leaders continue to take every occasion to reinforce the company's commitment to these values.

Here are three items drawn from the Goldman Sachs list:

- We stress teamwork in everything we do. While individual creativity is always encouraged, we have found that team effort often produces the best results.
- The dedication of our people to the firm and the intense effort they give their jobs are greater than one finds in most other organizations. We think that this is an important part of our success.
- We consider our size an asset that we try hard to preserve. We want to be big enough to undertake the largest project that any of our clients would contemplate, yet small enough to maintain the loyalty, the intimacy, and the esprit de corps that we all treasure and that contribute greatly to our success.

As Goldman has expanded in Europe, its leaders have labored to inculcate overseas staff with the company's value system and culture. I asked Fife for a progress report. "Is it working here in Europe?" he responded. "Yes and no. We're looking at thirty-five nationalities brought together over four years. Europeans are cynical until they realize you mean it, that this is not to be taken lightly. Initially . . . they didn't understand the seriousness with which the leaders developed these fundamental tenets of how we will work together in the firm." But the "yes" part of the story is strong. "We have made a lot of effort to teach people how to behave and act like Goldman Sachs people," Fife said. "Goldman Sachs's professional standards and values are the same throughout the world."

The Ocean Group, a British freight transport company, also started a transformation initiative by clarifying competing values and making its guiding principles explicit. The ultimate objective: to drive its change agenda deep within the organization to radically improve quality. The company's leader at the time, Nicholas Barber, assigned his top team to a series of monthly meetings. The group focused on the need for behavioral change. For six months, it explored the values implicit in the company culture and then crafted a new set of values more conducive to achieving Barber's ambition for the organization. At first, executives were uncomfortable discussing such a "soft" and personal topic. In time, the impact on performance of values became evident. Eventually, the executives committed themselves to changing the way people in the Ocean Group behaved, thereby changing the whole culture.

At one stage, Barber gave each employee yellow cards to be used when executives did not live up to company values. The procedure derived from the penalty system used in soccer. When the referees in a soccer game spot an infraction by a player, they "card" the player, using a yellow card to make the penalty visible to players on both teams, everyone in the stadium, and television viewers. It is both a strong signal and a warning, for the next card the referees assign is red, which expels a player from the match.

As Barber explained the idea, the Ocean Group's yellow cards were given to members of the executive team as well as other managers who ignored or betrayed the team's set of values. The card operated as feedback, with the intention of making the recipient think about his or her words or actions, and then, hopefully, to change. Barber encouraged the executive team to card him, and urged all employees to card their managers (which they did) if they deserved to be carded. Implicit in the card system were two assumptions of trust. Employees believed that the person carded did not intend to damage his or her peers, subordinates, or customers. At the same time, they assumed that the person "carding" was motivated by concern for a colleague and the organization, not pursuing a personal agenda.

Because trust, by definition, implies a relationship, it has to be mutual to be effective. Once it became evident that Barber and his top team were genuinely trying to enact the values every day in every interaction with customers, employees, and suppliers, the workforce followed suit. Barber succeeded in making new values an essential part of the way the Ocean Group does business because of the substantial energy devoted to crafting the values and the example set by the leader and his top team. Barber offered no illusions about the difficulties involved in changing his own behavior. Neither did Russell Seal, then chief executive officer of BP Oil, who also launched a major culture change in his organization.

Seal's goal was to shift BP Oil from its traditional command-and-control management style to create an environment in which business managers had greater authority and responsibility and had to deal with less bureaucracy. Seal told his aides that the implications of such a change would be enormous for everyone, including himself. In his habitual way of dealing with new business plans, Seal reviewed plans and then he composed twenty or more detailed questions to be asked of the relevant business managers. He expected the responses to be precise and promptly delivered. He still writes twenty to thirty questions (he says he can't stop himself after doing it for so many years), but instead of presenting the questions to his managers, he puts the paper in his drawer.

In the new culture, once a business plan is approved the business managers determine the success or failure of their plan. Seal supports and coaches his managers, but he no longer directs them.

In my work on values with leaders and organizations, I have observed a particular phenomenon: Service-oriented businesses, such as airlines and hotels, relate more readily to the importance of positive guiding principles. They seem better able to see the connection between guiding principles and performance than engineering or production-oriented organizations, such as computer manufacturers and automobile makers.

Next

The expression tells us that "talk is cheap." Yet if a meeting produces nothing but talk, that is, words, with no true exchange of ideas and opinions and no surfacing of real issues, talk can be expensive. Certainly, it wastes participants' time and energy, which could have been devoted to serious work. In addition, such a meeting represents a lost opportunity to move the group forward. The kind of talk that is essential to the organization's process of pursuing adaptive work is called dialogue.

Today the goal is not an imposed consensus that masks differences, so often thought to be the case. Rather, dialogue is intended to air differences so the group can benefit from everyone's ideas before reaching a conclusion. In the following chapter, I explain how dialogue can be fostered and what it can accomplish.

8

Promote Dialogue

ONE WORD DESCRIBES THE FOCUS and content of this chapter: dialogue.

Dialogue is not to be confused with debate. The word comes from the Greek *dialogos,* meaning "to break apart." It is about understanding other points of view and gaining insight into the underlying reasoning. Debate, on the other hand, is an attempt, through the use of argument, to convince another person of your point of view. I use the word *dialogue* to denote a serious exchange of disparate ideas, discourse that is intended to produce enlightenment but not necessarily agreement.

History is rich with examples of dialogue. Socrates, the fifth-century B.C. Greek philosopher, spent much of his life engaged in dialogues with students and passersby in the Athenian *agora,* or marketplace. His goal, not so different from mine, was to expose false beliefs and arrive at the truth.

In the ensuing pages, I show why dialogue is an essential element in the development of a new context: It identifies impediments to progress, such as competing values that threaten to derail a leader's ambition, and paves the way for collective solutions. I also show how leaders can use dialogue to inspire workers to make commitments to one another and to the new corporate ambition.

True dialogue represents a new kind of behavior and way of working for many organizations. Under management as we have known it, leaders emphasize debate followed by consensus. Too often, the consensus was not authentic and the agreement was disingenuous. Dialogue, however, serves to clarify positions or arguments on various sides of an issue. For dialogue to work optimally, participants must temporarily suspend judgment and illuminate all aspects of the different experiences, values, and assumptions that inform their arguments. In short, people engaged in dialogue seek to facilitate understanding—both their own and that of others—of numerous points of view. A shared awareness of diverse opinions and ideas is the goal.

When people enter a business discussion, they do so with diverse experiences, assumptions, and logic. There will be no shortage of opinions at a company that understands the imperative to change and grow. In my experience, the top team is usually divided at the beginning of most initiatives focused on change. As my friend and longtime colleague John Bray observes, a top "team" working together effectively may be an oxymoron along the lines of eternal youth and jumbo shrimp. We talk about all these things, but has anyone ever seen them?

What I do see repeatedly are well-meaning executives who think a change initiative is simply unnecessary. I have also encountered a dynamic I call "unconscious incompetence," wherein people agree intellectually, but fail to take effective action to make change happen. In other words, they are unable to alter their behavior to accommodate the new set of values that is needed to achieve success. Instead of recognizing or admitting their inability, they feign agreement, only to impede the plan through passivity. Part of the problem stems from the fact that people have a tendency to see problems in relation to their own experiences. But personality differences play a part, too.

Sometimes, executives resist new proposals for a reason more subtle and difficult to identify than a rigid reluctance to change. Deep down, they fear their own incompetence will reveal itself within a new system. When a company is growing rapidly, the people on the top team have a great stake in the past because they understand business relations far more than they do the future.

Contrast the creative, innovative manager, for example, with the controlling, overly rigid organizational man or woman. Whereas creative managers will for the most part, welcome the opportunity to explore new areas, equating that with freedom, the controlling manager will most likely have a very different response. For the latter personality, freedom means *escape* from innovation; innovation can be avoided. It is evident that these two personalities use a different vocabulary. Each may hear the words spoken by the other and by the leader, but certainly will not interpret them in the same way.

So why not just fire employees whose rigidity is hindering the establishment of the change initiative? Because companies need diversity to learn how to make better decisions. Jan Timmer of Philips Electronics, who labels the two competing camps "engineers" and "visionaries," recognizes that major change processes have both intellectual and emotional aspects. On the intellectual level, programs, milestones, and discipline are needed. At the emotional level, people need to invest their hearts and souls into the initiative.

Engineers consider it a waste of time to worry about "vision," and they scoff at "dreamers." They have a bias toward "fixing" the current important problem. According to Timmer, visionaries are more conceptual and entrepreneurial. They are long-term architects, dissatisfied with the status quo, who acknowledge that they cannot shape the future if they only control today's businesses. Timmer continues:

> Fire the engineers, and you get harmony and daydreaming—you need the cold shower of the numbers. Eliminate the visionaries and you have a financially control-oriented business without clear purpose or meaning in work for thousands of employees.
>
> Control-oriented people are highly suspicious. If something can't be measured, it is not meaningful. They place the organization above people. They give the impression they care about people but the spirit is usually missing. They love to talk about organization and strategy. They are more at ease with discussions about internal issues and structure. They are less at ease discussing the customer, people, and the mobilization of everyone in the organization toward a common goal.
>
> In a way, this creates an inevitable and not bad tension in which 100 percent consensus cannot be achieved. It's my job to manage diversity and different views in the company.

For Jan Carlzon of SAS, managing diversity and getting conflicting styles to productively interact is one of the most interesting missions in management. "It is not either/or but how to mingle these different perspectives. You need both," he told me, echoing Timmer. "When I let the innovators loose, our costs go out of control; when I invest too much authority in control-oriented people, they kill all innovation." Finding the right balance isn't easy. It won't, indeed can't, happen until dialogue occurs.

The purpose of dialogue is to enable each side of an argument to voice her or his viewpoint while working to understand the view of the other. The marketing vice president, for example, seeks to explore the underlying assumptions that the finance director brings to the meeting—and vice versa. Both parties try to understand the competing perspectives that influence how they operate. Inevitably, what they discover is that the source of the real conflict resides beneath the competing perspectives in the competing values. This is because it is *values* that determine perspective. Where competing values are at stake, dialogue is the only hope for resolution without alienating the participants.

Genuine dialogue can be an intimidating process, requiring time, intellectual energy, and courage. Participants may be reluctant to expose their vulnerabilities, say a weakness in knowledge, for fear of evoking their coworkers' disapproval. Perhaps someone fears that dialogue will reveal handicaps to progress within his or her own area.

The dialogue-based solution reflects the consensus of the participants and thus has their commitment, even if everyone does not completely or totally agree. Having learned collectively to think in a new way, dialogue participants have confidence in one another's support. The very process of ongoing dialogue means that old battles need not repetitively surface. Furthermore, it helps old-style leaders relinquish some authority and power within a supportive environment so that feelings of loss are minimal.

Effective leaders learn that their work includes identifying conflicts that impede the success of the business and bringing these conflicts into an open dialogue. The worst thing any leader can do is *not* address conflict in a way that is apparent. Different people cannot learn and solve problems mutually unless they understand the assumptions that underlie one another's positions. If the goal is a thoughtful decision regarding an appropriate course of action, listening and discussing, as opposed to heated argument, are wanted. The dialogue process is critical to improving the quality of decisionmaking and is central to the development of each individual on the team. Open disagreement is the only way real learning can take place at this level.

The process of building commitment through dialogue is gradual and systematic. Sometimes when the adaptive aspect of a solution is concerned, the commitment process is never quite inaugurated, because leaders fail to properly define the solution or the context, leaving a vacuum wherein operational concerns move in and take precedence over collective strategic action. Without commitment, managers focus on their functional roles; they pursue their own silo-minded agendas, which inevitably results in competition and conflict when cooperation is the aim. Factions emerge and dominant personalities rule functional fiefdoms. People remain loyal to their immediate bosses, not to the leadership's seemingly fuzzy or vague ideas.

Yet such problems need not be fatal, as I discovered in working with the fabrics division of Unilever, an Anglo-Dutch consumer products powerhouse. Lever Brothers Fabrics (LBF) was number two in an industry dominated by the Procter & Gamble Company. Striving to compete with P&G, LBF cut prices too far, and lost $100 million in a single year. Two new products fizzled, morale sagged, and growth stalled. Leaders felt that the company must, among other things, pay far more attention to details. Inattention was blamed for the profit loss. Its internal systems and controls were so weak, however, that senior managers had no time for anything beyond day-to-day concerns. Some managers felt almost proud of their ability to operate a plant built, as one put it, "with rubber bands."

Since LBF neglected to train junior people to handle details, senior managers spent an estimated 95 percent of their time on operations, leaving a mere 5 percent for strategic work. Moreover, rumors about both a potential merger and probable firings frightened many managers into keeping a low profile and avoiding risky projects. Refusing to remain passive, Paul Garwood, then the company's general manager, organized a twenty-person team and mandated it to identify the business's strategic challenge and to mobilize the company to meet that challenge. It was a stalwart effort, but the initiative went nowhere: Everyone was too busy coping with the present to ponder the future, much less commit to it. If they neglected the present, some argued, they would have no future.

When I began working with Garwood, I found his team deadlocked over its leadership agenda and unable to make use of one another as resources for solving problems together. Meetings were alternately dominated and demolished by various lone rangers who appeared to be so fascinated with their own opinions that they did not consider any of the fundamental questions needed to plan the company's future. This was not because Garwood's staff was insubordinate, which was not part of the company's culture. In fact, people on the team dutifully carried out Garwood's every order, but they drew the line when he asked for candor and creative thinking.

When Garwood impatiently pressed for reactions to proposals, most team members froze, either agreeing too easily or saying too little. Potential opponents became inattentive. The senior team muddled on, avoiding appropriate executive action by allowing itself to be distracted in a maze of operational trivia. Unwittingly, Garwood was creating roadblocks to dialogue. It was clear that Garwood would have to make some personal changes before he had any hope of engaging his company's best and brightest employees in a true dialogue.

As Xerox's John Seely Brown once wrote, "Each of us can send out signals—by raising our voices, squinting our eyes, stiffening our bodies—that block open conversation and shut people down." Brown resorted to videotaping important meetings to figure out exactly what signals he was unconsciously sending that could result in blocking dialogue.

Change is never easy, of course. Listen to Dee Hock, of Visa International, as he discusses the subject:

> We tend to fall in love with the things we think are true. We treasure those truths. . . . [T]hey are comfortable, and we can't bear to part with them, no matter how old or shabby or useless they become. But part with them we must, for our internal model of reality, our perspective, is a fun-house mirror: It distorts and discolors everything we see, learn, and experience. Perspective warps our perception and makes it difficult to view things accurately or conceive of them in new ways. It is the Achilles' heel of the mind.

Moreover, people who do not make changes usually try to force others to conform to their distorted perception. With that in mind, I advised Garwood to seek his teammates' *ideas,* not their acquiescence, among other things. Clearly, they needed encouragement from him to voice their opinions, to help their leader to refine his ideas and to help him discover better ones. I advised him to listen intently, offer praise frequently, and behave, literally, as a partner, merely the first among equals. I told him that, for every hour of reinforcing others' self-respect, he would receive ten hours of intelligent, committed collaboration. Indeed, he began to forge warm personal relationships outside the conference room with some of his formerly most entrenched opposition.

Garwood learned that change, as Dee Hock has observed, "is about seeing old things with new eyes—from different perspectives. . . . It's about reconceiving . . . a thought, a situation, a corporation, a product." When one does that, a whole new order is created.

One executive who could not bear Garwood's previous officiousness was amazed by his emerging trust in his colleagues. "I don't want to give up," she recalled him saying in a way that touched her. "We have to find a future together."

How Can One Promote Dialogue?

Here are some ideas:

See People as Individuals

Before leaders can successfully promote dialogue between competing factions in an organization, they must understand the perspectives from which individuals speak. The leader's first step toward establishing that understanding is an honest introspective self-analysis to evaluate how he or she views each member of the management team. In other words, the leader has to think of the people reporting to him or her as complex, multifaceted individuals. The leader is obligated to recognize the personality of people who are motivated by different (and I mean different from each other, as well as different from the leader) qualities, priorities, personal values, and lifestyles. Helpful to the leader is an astute awareness of strengths and weaknesses of team members so that these characteristics can be harvested or avoided, depending on the particular circumstances facing the company.

Gene Fife of Goldman Sachs told me that

There is no simple answer when it comes to human politics. . . . We have an army of bright people, the top of each class at Harvard, Stanford, and INSEAD. Some look for power, others wish to be recognized as experts, and some are intensively driven by money. The leader must want his people to succeed. Play to their strengths; different things for different people.

Sir Bryan Nicholson, former chairman of the British Post Office, shared with me his thought process for understanding and dealing with key individuals, which he describes as "managing by careful observation." Away from the chaos of the office, perhaps while lying in bed or soaking in the bath, Sir Bryan synthesizes issues in relationship to his top people, talking things out with himself and mentally laying out the arguments. In this way, he decides how to establish and nurture the trust that is the integral component of any effective discussion among people with diverse points of view.

In one case, Sir Bryan confided in one individual and gave him responsibility to address a key issue. He asked the employee to work at what he did best and personally found surrogates for other related tasks. As he moved along, Sir Bryan was careful not to intimidate or threaten this employee. Eventually, this individualized relationship rewarded Sir Bryan.

My longtime friend Bernard Fournier, former chief executive of Rank Xerox, goes even further in an effort to view his team members as individuals. During the twenty years I have known him, I have been continually struck by the level of intimacy he cultivates with colleagues on his team. Much of Bernard's personal and social agenda involves them. More often than not, when my wife and I are invited to his home, we are joined by members of his current team or people with whom he has worked in the past. A natural warmth and friendliness characterizes each and every evening we spend in his company. Referring to his team, Bernard told me that "we get to know each other. You need *friends* to get things done."

Uncover Negative Patterns of Relationships

Sir Bryan Nicholson, who acknowledges that the frameworks of relationships are difficult to break once patterns are established, compares them to sexual relationships. "Whatever position two people adopt in the first month, it doesn't change very much in the course of their relationship." Though difficult to break, they are not impossible to change. A leader can turn things around by encouraging introspection and self-reflection on both sides. Sir Bryan describes what happened to him and one of his team members during the transformation at the British Post Office:

In my case, my desire to avoid conflict among individuals on the team led me to intervene in conflict situations too frequently and too early. Another executive had to fundamentally change his behavior from a contentious, controlling style to one of more consensus and using his colleagues as resources. Helping him to achieve this was one of my greatest accomplishments. We had to develop an open acceptance that none of us was perfect. We learned to laugh at our imperfections and respect the way each of us does things.

Deconstructing negative relationships allows for positive dialogue.

Enable and Encourage Feedback

"Unconscious incompetence needs to be dealt with by learning from mistakes and going back to explain the problem and the consequences," Bernard Fournier points out. "It is critical to get people convinced about the objectives, the way of working, and the values." But how can a leader facilitate this learning process? Fournier advises:

Build an informal and open way of getting things on the table. That means feedback. My team gives feedback to me and we give feedback to each other. At one level, this is via a formal structure related to specific behaviors which we have argued about, and it's reviewed collectively every six months. We also give each other feedback on "the way we work" in the course of everyday problem solving and decision making.

This awareness, he concluded, "allows us to work more effectively as a team and resolve business problems [about] which we may have differing perspectives more effectively."

Keep Everyone in the Work

The leader must guarantee the legitimacy of the dialogue by eliminating "work avoidance"—that is, closing off escape routes that different people use to avoid confronting important, often deeply divisive, issues. The leader has to put the work back in the group, creating conditions within which the dialogue can continue. Still, it may be necessary for the leader alone to decide what the appropriate course of action must be.

At Johnson & Johnson, Ralph Larsen is known as a leader who gives people a comfortable forum in which to air concerns, share ideas, and discuss differences. In short, he promotes dialogue by creating the kind of atmosphere in which people can do the work that they must do. The executive conferences he sponsored are one way that he literally closes off escape routes to work avoidance. Here is how one participant, Bill Nielsen, describes one of J&J's FrameworkS sessions:

> You were cooped up and made a part of the executive committee, and everybody who was in the room had all the same rights. It is stripping away all the titles . . . opening up the ranks . . . and embracing the idea that nobody has all the answers, and we're not sure who has the right answer, so . . . we've got to decide together and take counsel.

This is not to say that Larsen relinquishes control. Quite the contrary. "He is a decision maker," Nielsen clarifies. "He promotes talking things out and tries to build consensus. But only so long, and then, when he gets an idea regarding what the right answer is, if that idea isn't being made, he'll say, 'here's the way I see it.'"

It goes without saying that the leader must be prepared to invest a good deal of time and effort in managing conflicts and promoting dialogue on significant issues. This is the only way in which the team will be able to understand alternative perspectives. It is the only way people at this level can learn about and become committed to something outside of their prior experiences.

Far too often, executives devote large amounts of time to getting the answer (strategy), and too little time to determining the organization's learning needs, which will enable the strategy's effective implementation in the various areas of responsibility. Too little time is spent getting everyone in the organization concentrating on the same goal. Promoting dialogue goes a long way toward remedying this shortcoming, but that requires a leader who is a highly effective listener. The superior leader is one who knows how to reveal the root causes of important issues, and simultaneously encourage team members to use each other as resources (not competitors) in the problem-solving process.

Next

In Dee Hock's experience, change can be both exhilarating and terrifying, because in a deep sense, "you are questioning your very identity and sense of value." Despite the fear, the founder of Visa concluded by saying: "Take the risk. It's worth it!"

Indeed it is, but leaders may doubt that advice when they are in the midst of the stressful process of working through the adaptive component of a solution. Chances are, stress is increasing for everyone else too. Stress has its uses, but only in moderation. One must find the very delicate balance between productive stress and stress that obstructs one's ability to function.

As I discuss in the next chapter, a leader must learn to regulate the stress level within the workforce by finding ways to release pressure when it becomes too intense but to turn up the heat if he or she senses that people are becoming too complacent. One of the most delicate tasks of a leader is learning to gauge just the right level of disequilibrium to produce the required change.

9

Regulate Distress

FOR MANY YEARS, one of the most effective ways of cooking speedily was to use a pressure cooker. The pressure from steam builds up heat and cooks food more quickly, invariably producing a flavorful dish. The disadvantage, as many an absent-minded cook discovered, is that the pot can explode if it is not watched carefully.

A pressure cooker is an apt analogy for a business in the midst of adaptive work. Progress occurs when heat and pressure are combined to produce the results the company desires. Without heat and pressure, nothing would be accomplished. But a word of warning is appropriate here: Too much pressure on a workforce can lead to paralysis, and then nothing gets done properly, if at all. People become anxious and exhausted so that a simple choice between, say, Grape Nuts or raisin bran for breakfast seems overwhelming. On the other hand, too little pressure can lead to complacency. It is the leader's responsibility to maintain a delicate balance between too much and not enough stress. Alert to the process, they add heat when necessary or, conversely, release steam when too much pressure builds up.

To some degree, stress or distress is inevitable for employees in the pressure cooker. They are being asked to change their attitudes and styles of performing jobs, which have become second nature. As fundamental changes take place in the company, new incoming values mandated by adaptive work are likely to conflict with the organization's traditional outgoing values. Jobs may be redesigned or eliminated, new responsibilities assigned, and valued and productive friendships dissolved to benefit a plan that seems obscure and a future that feels uncertain.

When the distress level gets too high, people become psychologically paralyzed. We have all had this experience, poised on the precipice between raisin bran and Grape Nuts, feeling that we cannot deal with one more thing, no matter how simple it may appear to be. In business, stress-induced paralysis is counterproductive in every way. When distress reaches a certain level, a person can neither learn (in fact, he or she temporarily loses the cognitive capacity to take in and process more information) nor perform even close to his or her former capacity.

Leaders cannot afford to ignore the symptoms of such psychological dislocation. They must make adjustments, distinguishing between too much distress and too little. They must recognize, too, that sometimes distress is caused by the employee's misperception of the leader's real role. A particular employee may be experiencing an uncomfortably high level of stress because he or she is under the erroneous impression that the leader will readily solve every problem. They are waiting for instructions rather than mobilizing people who have the collective skills to solve the problem.

When people first experience new pressure and distress, all eyes turn for help to the leader. "Fix the situation. Pull another rabbit out of the hat. Restore order. I have put my hope and trust in you," their appeals seem to say. If the company is to realize its new ambition and firmly establish a new context, how-

ever, the leader must resist the impulse to offer immediate re-
lief, because that seductively familiar behavior can lead to complacency. Paradoxically, the leader's work includes maintaining a
certain level of disequilibrium, which is necessary to the process
of real change.

Sir Bryan Nicholson recalls an incident at the British Post Office when two people who reported directly to him were locked
in a fierce battle over a specific business issue. He started to intervene, interpreting one executive's message to the other in a
well-intentioned but misguided attempt to restore equilibrium.
He soon discovered that it was more important and helpful to
allow the conflict to take its natural course so that the underlying issues could surface. Candidly, Sir Bryan confessed that he
intervened in the first place because he does not like conflict.
Just as the employees he manages needed to learn to live and sit
still with conflict to maintain a healthy level of disequilibrium,
so did Sir Bryan.

If the leader tries to maintain calm at all costs, he or she loses
the opportunity to learn and issues an invitation to complacency, the archenemy of any corporate transformation. Sapping
energy and blocking learning, complacency will surely overtake
a workforce unless the leader firmly keeps the distress level high
enough to avoid it. Paralysis and complacency are twin symptoms of a leader's failure to regulate distress.

Andrew S. Grove, the respected chairman of Intel Corporation of Cupertino, California, the globe's top maker of integrated circuits, prefers the word "fear" rather than "distress," but
his meaning is the same. Grove believes that the most important
role of a leader "is to create an environment in which people are
passionately dedicated to winning in the marketplace. Fear
plays a major role in creating and maintaining such passion.
Fear of competition, fear of bankruptcy, fear of being wrong, and
fear of losing, all can be powerful motivators." The aim, as

Grove sees it, is to cultivate the right level of fear in employees. He wants them to fear losing. He wants them to be alert to the possibility that some day, any day, some development in the environment will change the rules of the game. He wants fear to be a survival instinct in his employees.

Grove also wants to regulate the kinds of fear his employees experience. Middle managers, for example, must not fear that they will be punished for carrying bad news—Grove's management will not shoot the messenger. Fears that prevent people from voicing their ideas, articulating their convictions, and sharing their observations are poisonous. Nothing can be more detrimental to the well-being of a company than employees who are afraid to speak up. That is, unless we are referring to a complete absence of fear. Grove reaches this conclusion from his personal experience and psychological introspection. Fear, he says, makes him scan his e-mail every day; fear gives him the will to listen to bad news without interrupting when he really wants to say, "Everything is all right, the sky is not falling."

Adaptive work as a whole can and, indeed, should create a certain amount of distress in the workforce. Exacerbating the feeling of stress is its unpredictability. Since adaptive work does not simply march along in time to a constant beat, neither can the stress that is inherent in parts of it. During the process of the company's transformation, distress will be evoked in different people at different times under varying circumstances. Therefore, leaders cannot monitor only the solution's overall progress. They must also remain aware of stress in the workforce as a whole, and individually as new initiatives are introduced. Herein lies the real work of leaders. They must cultivate a balcony view and watch the details unfold on the field. It is their responsibility to regulate distress, increasing and decreasing the heat and pressure, depending on the circumstances.

The decision to alter the role of middle managers, as we discussed in an earlier chapter, triggers distress for both managers and their supervisees. Managers will feel that they have lost authority, whereas workers will suddenly be expected to assume authority, making decisions they did not make before. Yet the nature of distress the two groups experience is unlikely to be the same; managers are apt to feel fear and anger, whereas their former supervisees are likely to feel confused and nervous about job expectations. In such a circumstance, the leader needs to be careful not to let the manager's distress level reach the point of paralysis or allow the other group's confusion to lead to complacency. In other words, the leader's work to understand and regulate employees' distress is a complicated process; it is incumbent upon him or her to simultaneously act selectively and cautiously—and boldly and quickly.

Regulating distress must be performed on an individualized, case-by-case basis. Responsible leaders, aware of potential conflicts from adaptive work, are cognizant of situations in which the level of distress can become too high or too low for the well-being of the company. Leaders must, as my colleague Ron Heifetz likes to say, "hear the song beneath the words."

Sometimes a leader must create a "burning platform," a crisis mentality, to move an initiative forward. For instance, SAS always seems to be in crisis and manages to make money. British Airways, on the other hand, always seems to maintain a state of calm, yet somehow always loses money.

Pursuing the task of regulating distress, Ron Heifetz suggests that one should distinguish between issues or situations that are "ripe" and "unripe." Heifetz considers an issue to be ripe when there is a "general urgency for action" that is felt throughout the company. An issue is unripe when the urgency is local, limited to a single area of management or workforce. Ripe issues—

widespread complacency during adaptive work, for example, are easier to pursue than unripe issues, such as when signs of paralysis appear in the assembly line.

In the pages ahead, I show how some of our most successful companies have set about the task of using distress to keep workers, as Heifetz puts it, "in a productive discomfort zone." I also offer my expertise on how that can be accomplished in a company.

How Does One Regulate Distress?

Create an environment that recognizes that time is required for adaptive learning. Yet speed is required as well in order to fulfill an ambition.

A leader must prioritize, sequence, and pace the work. If leaders respond to pressure by declaring that *everything* is critical, or if they begin new initiatives without slowing down or stopping others, they run the risk of overwhelming employees. An insightful leader knows how (and when) to protect people by regulating the pace of change. That means you avoid launching four innovations at a time when one or two have a better chance of being successful.

At British Airways, for example, Sir Colin Marshall paced the company's shift from an internal focus to a customer focus over a two- to three-year period. Important issues were dealt with one at a time, rather than all at once. By setting deadlines that may not have appeared reasonable, but could be achieved, and calculating an appropriate pace for instituting changes, Sir Colin allowed employees at all levels of the company to learn what and how they needed to change without becoming overwhelmed at the prospect. Remember that everyone, at one time or another, felt overwhelmed, but Sir Colin's approach fostered feelings of mutual trust and cohesiveness.

The inability to slow or stop previous initiatives is human nature, plain and simple. Executives have a hard time pulling the plug on projects they previously sanctioned. Meanwhile, they keep adding new initiatives without stopping any old ones, not only stretching their own capabilities to the limit (and often beyond), but also those of overworked subordinates who are asked to deliver on yet another "priority."

I have suggested to two or three organizations I have worked with that they reduce current programs, initiatives, and activities by 30 percent. If, in theory, senior management agrees in theory, in practice they simply cannot cut the umbilical cord. It is rare to find an organization with an established screening system that mandates, "if we add this, we'll take away that." Simply put, most organizations neither know which projects to stop nor how to go about assessing which projects to stop. To help leaders sort through a glut of initiatives, I advise them to imagine that they are part of a leveraged buyout team that just bought their business. Then they must ask themselves which initiatives could reasonably be expected to continue once the buyout is completed.

Give people a way to measure their progress.

A key to good leadership is to figure out the correct level of pressure for employees so they work at their full potential and remain focused on their work. Unless people have guideposts to know how they are doing, they will be unable to concentrate on critical issues that ultimately will determine the initiative's success or failure. "In the end you need a process, not control," according to Russell Seal of BP Oil. "If I have learned anything in twenty-five years of managing in a large organization, it is that instructions don't work." Defining and setting the right measures are key to adaptive change, particularly when customer responsiveness is the goal.

A case in point is Ford Motor Company's Jim O'Connor, who believes that "everything must have a standard. Without that, we will not know if we are improving." To measure progress during its overhaul of customer service, Ford established measurable standards in every process. For example, O'Connor explains that "we focused on 'live in 5 in 95'—that is, 95 percent of the time the phone is answered within five rings. [W]e measured calls abandoned (not answered)." The company also set standards for delivering emergency parts (twenty-four hours) and responding to written requests or complaints (three days).

By setting up specific processes for measuring employees' progress in meeting individual goals, the company is applying pressure for the purpose of improvement. At the same time, it eases the pressure from anxiety that builds when people have no idea whether or not they are meeting expectations. Concrete numbers, good or bad, can reenergize the effort. ("Hey, keep pushing. We are almost there." Or conversely, "We've got to try harder. We are falling behind.")

Create, in the words of British psychoanalyst D. W. Winnicott, a "holding environment."

Central to the leader's role is the creation of conditions that facilitate people's best work. These conditions may include a psychological ambience in which people feel secure or safe enough to voice disagreements with, and question, the need for the changes they are in the midst of. Or it can be an actual physical space in which people from various parts of the organization can work collaboratively in a nonjudgmental atmosphere. In any event, a holding environment is necessary if a leader hopes to develop cooperation within an entire organization. It encourages uninhibited and open dialogue among employees about the challenges they face. It also allows them to express pride and enthusiasm for the contributions they are making toward company success.

Recall KPMG, where Ruud Koedijk appointed 100 explorers to evaluate the old corporate culture, define the values of a new culture, and determine where similarities exist. They carried out their assignments in a physical work space they established in a separate location. They arrived each day in casual attire (removing their neckties seemed to ease the pressure), and created a psychological environment where ideas took precedence over hierarchy. The holding space allowed them to develop collectively as emissaries adept at articulating to colleagues the values of the new culture at KPMG.

Colin Marshall defined such a psychological space at British Airways by encouraging employees to take initiative, permitting them to perform as individuals, and fostering their efforts to communicate their experiences with each other in a collaborative effort to solve BA's problems. Similarly, Jan Timmer says that "encouraging the people" was central to his work of regulating stress so that it did not overwhelm the Philips employees. Timmer recommends:

Involve everyone in the debate. . . . Focus everyone on the external environment. Encourage initiatives. Generate thousands of small projects and encourage healthy competition, and visibly reward the successes. . . . I am more convinced than ever of the "bottom-up" approach. The leader must represent people in the frontline, build on enthusiasm, and share practical examples.

Protect voices of leadership that lack authority.
Sometimes these voices speak at the wrong time and with too much passion. Because passion adds even more intensity to the turmoil, other participants may turn to the leader and say, "shut him up." If that happens, the leader must resist censoring the voice, because it may offer valuable insight. A leader's real work is to listen to those voices, disharmonious as they may be, and

discover what they say, since he or she may not hear it else-where. Resisting a natural impulse to quash an opposing view-point, the leader has to climb to the balcony, survey the enterprise from the perspective of the dissenting voice, and ask, "What is the alternative viewpoint that this person is advancing? Why is it important to listen to it? Is there something I'm miss-ing?"

Robert Haas, chief executive officer of Levi Strauss & Com-pany, may wish he and his managers had paid closer attention to the voices of retailers who tried to tell them that the venerable old brand of blue jeans was fading in all the wrong places. En-grossed in his dream of turning the company into a model of en-lightened management practices and concurrently involved in a major reengineering effort, Haas somehow lost touch with the marketplace and the fickle tastes of youth. Even when people on the front lines reported what they were seeing, Levi Strauss's management, in the words of one distributor, "didn't want to be-lieve." Now, it is sales that are fading. Levi's estimated market value is in a free fall and the company is scrambling to recap-ture at least a share of its old-time glory.

Safeguard people who raise hard questions, generate distress, and call attention to the organization's internal contradictions. Since they do not have authority, these people often have the liberty and capacity to provoke further analysis of decisions made by that authority. A cautionary note: It is easy for such people to become scapegoats, particularly in an atmosphere where tension is already running high. Make it clear to middle managers, who will feel the most threatened by criticism from the rank-and-file, that all opinions are welcome.

Ask people to identify their own adaptive challenges.

Many individuals are asked to change every time a company confronts a challenge. They must reflect upon the most appro-priate adaptive challenges and subsequent actions to take.

Leaders must help people see themselves, undefensively, both as part of the problem and part of the solution. Employees must be encouraged to ask: What can I do? How can I add my unique value to the effort? What managerial habits do I need to unlearn? Whether leaders assume this responsibility themselves or enlist the assistance of a task force, as Ruud Koedijk did at KPMG, the objective is the same: to be available in the role of counselor or coach to people in the organization as they undertake the process of changing behaviors and unlearning old habits that can block organizational growth.

Next

Among the most critical and productive actions a leader can take is to give employees, regardless of their positions in the company, the feeling that they have the freedom to take responsibility. A leader must encourage employees to use initiative, think for themselves, and make decisions rather than passively waiting to be told what to do. As the next chapter emphasizes, a policy in which almost all employees throughout a company assume more responsibilities stretches the skills of the workforce and rewards big dividends in terms of overall performance.

10

Make Everyone
Collectively Responsible

THIS CHAPTER ASSERTS that leaders must encourage people to assume responsibility, and then give work back to those who need to do the changing. I will discuss what leaders can do to facilitate an environment designed to help employees undertake the processes of learning and unlearning, prerequisites to successfully taking on more responsibility. I agree with Jim P. Manzi, former chairman and chief executive officer of the Lotus Development Corporation, when he once observed: "We are smarter than me."

In traditional businesses, leaders establish policies and procedures that are communicated to workers and enforced by middle managers. Workers follow orders, and when a new situation arises, they seek the advice of managers. Today, more and more leaders recognize the severe limitations that this arrangement places on the most important resources a company possesses—the knowledge, skills, and initiative of its employees. When a company confronts a strategic problem, it needs to be able to rely on these resources.

Many leaders have responded by reconceptualizing the ways in which their organizations make decisions. They encourage those best equipped to solve problems to do so. As Larry Bossidy of AlliedSignal has said, "It's not a platitude to say that you have to utilize people's brains and imagination and dedication. They know their jobs better than you do."

But, what I am talking about is more than redistributing responsibility. Problems are often crossfunctional, so the locus of responsibility is not clearly defined; this means that the real work of leaders includes instilling an attitude in managers that encourages them "to catch loose balls and run with them," so to speak. In other words, those who perform the work must also be responsible for framing the work; leaders must help employees adapt their working styles toward this end. A critical piece of all of this is, of course, unlearning. Because until old ways are cast aside, no one will be able to move forward.

Senior leaders, middle managers, and frontline workers are accustomed to operating under the old command-and-control system, making the most of their individual roles. Unlearning that style of control is not the only change leaders need to make. They need to make a transition away from certain deeply held beliefs and unstated assumptions that have been governing their choices and behavior. Recognize that leadership is performed every day by many people throughout the organization. As J&J faced the challenge of becoming e-enabled, it needed to confront assumptions, including those related to the implications of decentering decision. All of a sudden, people are asked to discard the habits of a lifetime and to give up the only way of working they have ever known. The time had come to make such a transformation, however. Successful leaders recognized that we had gone from a command-and-control leadership model to what *World Link* magazine calls "a command and connect" leadership model.

Paul Garwood encountered such a situation at the Unilever fabrics division. Faced with a culture that, despite aspirations to the contrary, did not encourage creativity or innovation and was always playing second fiddle to Procter & Gamble, Garwood's challenge was to engender a collective confidence throughout the division that would motivate people to use their expertise and ideas to create and implement a winning strategy. He believed it was time they took responsibility for their own future. Before such radical changes could be instituted, the Unilever employees had to discard doubts and insecurities that kept them from doing their best work.

What did Garwood do to turn negative images into positive ones? First, he widened people's horizons by providing a week-long seminar in which employees were taught new concepts and approaches in strategy from professors from Harvard Business School and INSEAD. Volunteers committed to learning about emerging customer needs traveled to the Far East; others visited labs studying the future at MIT in Cambridge, Massachusetts; still others went to labs in California. Garwood dedicated a separate area in the building for their work. Finally, he moved around asking questions without providing answers, offered resources and support, and encouraged people in their work. In short, Garwood created conditions that enabled his employees to do their work. This meant helping them emerge from a collective depression induced by the constant disappointment of never being in first place. They had to unlearn the psychological state of second-class citizen. Most important, Garwood helped his team understand and shed the fear of failure, because they could succeed only if they were willing to risk failure.

When Jan Carlzon took over SAS's Vingresor subsidiary he was still in his early thirties. He remembers fearing that he "wouldn't be accepted and afraid that he would fail." Like other young, inexperienced managers, Carlzon assumed a persona that mirrored his perception of a boss and he acted the way he thought a boss should.

> "I straightened my tie and summoned my staff," he recalls. "One after another trooped into my office, and I issued firm instructions about what was to be done: 'Change that timetable!' 'Make a deal with that hotel!'" What Carlzon describes as management by edict became the order of the day, no matter what the situation.
>
> What I was going through was, no doubt, what most of us experience the first time we find ourselves in the spotlight. I began behaving differently because I was acting out the role I believed I'd been given.
>
> I assumed that everyone at Vingresor expected me to be able to do everything better than they could, and that I should make all the decisions.

Lacking the wisdom that came with experience, but quick with solutions for everyone else's problems, Carlzon admits that he made countless decisions with inadequate information.

Yet it was a lesson Carlzon, like all leaders, had to learn more than once. Years later, in the top position at SAS, he asked the people in the company's air cargo division to develop a new strategy. Disappointed by their response, he sat down with the cargo operations manager and said, "This can't be so difficult. What the market wants, of course, is door-to-door service. Develop such a product." Although he was obeyed, the campaign was a disaster.

> I . . . made a decision from the top of the pyramid about an aspect of the business that was completely unfamiliar to me. I lacked a basic knowledge of the cargo market's special structure and division of labor. [Had] I . . . created an atmosphere in which the cargo manager's own ideas flourished, the mistake would not have been made. Instead, I took

the easy way out, opting to decide myself, even though I didn't know what I was doing.

Philip J. Carroll, Jr., chairman and chief executive officer of Fluor Corporation, described an experience concerning his tenure at Shell Oil Company. Before coming to Shell, Carroll's only experience as a leader had been in the military, the quintessential exemplar of command-and-control management. When he arrived at Shell, he found the same sort of system in operation. It suited him well until he confronted its inherent deficiency. "Maybe if I had given these people more leeway," Carroll remembers, "maybe if I hadn't dictated the answer in the early stages, we would have come to a better solution."

Reaching that conclusion, Carroll was able to make major changes in the giant corporation. Along the way, he taught his colleagues a crucial lesson: People cannot "really feel responsible or accountable unless they are free." Put another way, employees will not work enthusiastically if they are expected simply to obey orders. Having no input into decisions regarding one's work will lead to apathy regarding its outcome.

The General Executive Office, or GEO, made up of the president and three executive vice presidents, made virtually every decision of any consequence for the enormous Shell company, including budget decisions. Each year, division leaders came before the GEO to ask the parent company to invest $1 billion on this oil field or $1 billion on that refinery. In the oil industry, projects of such major magnitude take years to work out, so the person who proposed the idea was frequently gone by the time results were compiled, meaning no one was accountable.

Carroll broke divisions into much smaller units, each with its own board of directors. When their officers appealed to the GEO, Carroll told them: "Look, your dividend requirement is fixed, and that's determined by your capital deployed. And you've got debt. Now, if you want to make that next investment, it's not my decision, it's yours. Can you meet your dividend payment and finance it, or is your debt going to go up?"

Carroll was helping his managers learn how to frame their problems and then adapt and learn how to work and deliver results in this new environment. He was helping them to adapt. Given the freedom to run their own shops, leaders of the smaller units stopped caring as much about receiving a big infusion of corporate cash, and started to care more about the financial sense of what they were contemplating. Suddenly, there was accountability.

A postscript: During a long interview with Carroll while he was still president and chief executive officer of Shell, I asked him how he felt about ceding decisionmaking power to those hired to do the work. Here is what he told me:

> If you're really honest with yourself, you start out in a company feeling that every job you have is, to some important extent, about how you're going to get to that next star. When you get into a position where you know with high certainty that this is the end of the line, you start thinking about—I know it sounds corny—about what kind of legacy you're going to leave in the company.
>
> That makes you think and look at things very differently. I spent a lot of time reflecting and reading about that in the months before becoming CEO. The truth is, there is a high level of ambiguity about it. But you do have to have certain underlying assumptions, premises about the direction you're going. If you have total ambiguity, total uncertainty about what's right or wrong, I think you don't have a hope.

Carroll believes that leaders should be realistic on the subject of their own limitations: how many times they are right, how many times they are wrong. (Remember, as I cited in Chapter 8

Dee Hock labeled misperception as the "Achilles' heel of the mind.") As Carroll notes, a leader must be willing to say, "Look, other people have good ideas as well. And if I'm going to be the one calling all the shots, then the company is probably going to be batting pretty low."

As for Phil Carroll's legacy? Bringing more people into the decisionmaking process is the key to corporate success in his view. "So a big part of my legacy, I think, will be that I got more people involved, and getting more people involved raised the level of quality." I submit that that kind of reflection is the real work of leaders.

To achieve goals with "stretch," leaders must follow Carroll's example by engaging more managers in the process of understanding the external environment and in defining what the company requires—competencies, capabilities, and values—to move ahead. Ultimately, the adaptive process, which at its root is dependent on individuals sharing a set of values or "culture," leads people to experience confidence and trust in each other, which in turn allows them to move toward the goal of discovering and implementing innovative solutions to new and old problems.

As first-rate leaders like Carroll know well, a leader's vision alone is no longer enough. To achieve real change, leaders must enlist managers to take responsibility for implementing the strategy. Leaders do this by promoting dialogue, which enables employees at all levels to understand the logic that underlies the proposed initiatives. From there, people can move toward adopting the values that will motivate their interactions.

When Jan Carlzon became president of SAS's affiliate, Linjeflyg, in 1981, the company was awash in red ink. From the beginning, he preached the importance of employees taking the initiative and assuming more responsibility. He called a meeting in the airline's main hangar for Linjeflyg workers from all over

Sweden. Standing on a ladder fifteen feet above the crowd, Car-lzon announced, "This company is not doing well. It's losing money." He went on to say that, despite the fact that he was Linjeflyg's new president, he knew nothing about it and "can't save the company alone."

"The only chance for Linjeflyg to survive is if you help me—assume responsibility yourselves, share your ideas and experiences so we have more to work with. I have some ideas of my own, and we'll probably be able to use them. But most important, you are the ones who must help me, not the other way around."

The people, who had expected Carlzon to tell them what *he* was going to do, were surprised and impressed. He clarified his rationale: These were the people closest to the company's customers—that is, they were in a better position than he to identify what customers needed and wanted and to spot changes in the market. (Or as Larry Bossidy puts it, "They know their jobs better than you do.")

Carlzon uses soccer as an analogy to discuss the relationships among leader, manager, and frontline worker. The coach is the leader, responsible for picking the strongest players and establishing an environment that allows them to play their best. The team captain, like the manager, is out on the field with the team calling plays. During the action, when the situation changes by the second, however, individual players on the front line decide how to win the game.

Middle managers have been "scape-goated" for years. "Eighty percent of them are not strong or lack self-confidence," one executive told me. "This is the central trap. It results in middle managers not being trusted. The system will eat them if they make a mistake so they don't do anything." The middle managers aren't to blame; their leaders are. The real work of leaders is to instill an attitude that allows the managers to say with confidence, "I can assume responsibility for problems that touch me. I can frame the issues and make sure the work is accomplished."

I have long suspected that the primary role of the middle manager is to deliver the budget. If he doesn't do it, who will? I sense that in most organizations there is a silent handshake between the chief executive officer and middle management, in which the chief executive is saying, you deliver the budget and *then* do whatever you can to improve customer responsiveness. As one middle manager said to me, "If I don't achieve my customer satisfaction targets, I get yelled at. If I don't achieve my budget, I get fired."

"I have a jaundiced view of middle management," Peter Bijur, chairman and chief executive officer of Texaco, told me. "There is a generation gap as well as middle management mediocrity. I don't understand the motivation of the next generation. We are all in a business in a crisis. I'm here from 7 A.M. to 7 P.M. and they leave at 4 P.M. for softball. When it comes to problem solving, they have a 'What do you want me to do, boss?' mentality."

Middle managers seems to be caught in the midst of a sea change in management style. They lack the confidence required to give up their old role and have no motive for relinquishing their power over the frontline people. It is time for leaders to change all that.

In Jan Carlzon's rush to implement the adaptive component of his solution and save the company, he focused on the front line, with impressive early results, but he bypassed the team captains, the middle managers. At first, Carlzon says, he did not notice that they were confused and angry. Suddenly, they found themselves " squeezed" rather than "squeezing." For reasons managers did not understand, frontline workers were demanding their help, whereas management was ordering them to do things they had never done before. When managers were told to "support" the efforts of the front line, they interpreted that as a demotion.

Carlzon offers an example. He arrived at the SAS terminal in Stockholm to find hundreds of passengers racing about in search of the luggage carousels. The electric monitors that match carousels and flight numbers were not working. When Carlzon went to the information booth, the woman on duty told him she had already suggested to her manager that they put up handwritten signs. The manager would not listen and insisted that the problem would be solved momentarily. That had been a week before. Shortly thereafter, Carlzon offered the manager a choice: Move down to the terminal floor where he could make on-the-spot decisions, or keep his office, but hand over the authority to make decisions to the people on the floor.

How does on-site decisionmaking work in practice? Suppose a middle manager sets a challenge: Workers are to get all of the suitcases from a flight onto the conveyor belts before the passengers reach the carousel to retrieve them. The ramp employees accept the challenge, but say they need seven extra workers and three additional trucks to do the job. It then becomes the middle manager's task to find the extra people and equipment.

In a traditional company, the middle manager would simply turn down the proposal because the additional personnel and trucks were not in the budget. In a company where customer responsibility is everyone's bailiwick, the middle manager, assuming the goal is important enough, juggles his budget or overspends it, in the expectation that the improved results will cover his bet. In such an organization, the locus of responsibility resides in those who can do the work, and managers are right there to catch the loose balls I spoke of earlier. Almost any company can imitate this approach.

Enlightened leaders allow good ideas to emerge from the workforce and, then, choose which ones to support. In this way, they are "leading" not only by fostering and lending credibility to other people's good ideas, but, in addition, they are nurturing the process that encourages employees to think creatively. Whether the broad objectives are conceptualized at the top, then handed down, or are developed from ideas originating with the workforce, once they become initiatives, middle management divides them into a set of smaller objectives that frontline people can accomplish. At that point, the middle manager's role changes from administrative to supportive. In other words, on their own turf frontline people decide how to seize opportunities and resolve problems, and middle managers enable them to do so. The work now resides where it belongs, with those who can best accomplish it.

How Can One Make Everyone Responsible?

Here are some of the lessons mastered by business leaders with whom I have worked.

Resist the temptation to supply answers.

When you hand over a problem to someone, do not suggest your own ideas for its solution. Even a hint can set in motion the old, learned response you are working to overcome. People are trained to seek out the boss's desired solution. Even the best-intentioned leader has to be on guard against inadvertently tripping the switch that will send employees off on a hunt to do what they think the boss wants done.

The real work of leaders involves setting the context and framing the problem to be solved. In addition, good leaders ask the right questions to focus or guide people as they grapple with issues and develop solutions. When employees design solutions, it may be surprising to learn that it is not the leader's role to accept or reject. Far from it. Instead, he or she should encourage dialogue to evaluate all potential solutions, thus helping people explore the underlying logic of various competing perspectives that often exist. Thus the leader draws more people—and their knowledge and intelligence—into the decisionmaking process. Unlike technical solutions, at this stage it is necessary to let the issues "cook." Certainly, in technical work, when the CEO knows the answer, it is his or her responsibility to convey that answer. But, when the challenge is adaptive, successful leaders understand that the most powerful position is sometimes that of "consultant."

In this vein, Jeffrey B. Swartz, president and chief executive officer of the Timberland Company, once related a wonderful story about how the company finally came to have a day-care center, years after his own attempt to get one going had failed. "A woman asked me what I was going to do about day care," wrote Swartz, whose company is based in Stratham, New Hampshire. "I told her that I was not going to do anything . . . my kids are getting older, and they don't need day care."

A stunned silence followed what sounded to everyone like a callous reply. But Swartz didn't stop there. He added that if the employee needed day care and if her colleagues supported the idea, she should let him know what *she* wanted to do about it. And she did. She organized a group that polled employees on the issue, researched the cost of a program, and identified where the funding would come from. Then she scheduled a meeting to present the group's case to Swartz. When the boss asked why she had invited him to the meeting, she noted, without missing a beat, "To applaud." And he did, loudly. "That meeting was spectacular!" Swartz explained. "The way the group tackled the problem [was] amazing. All I did was to move out of the way."

To be sure, it is usually not easy for a leader to keep his or her hands off. For traditional leaders, who are used to the command-and-control approach, old ways have to be unlearned. Even nontraditional leaders may find they have to change.

Denis Tunnicliffe, managing director of London Underground Ltd., states unequivocally that "the best stuff comes out of teamwork," and enabling that teamwork is "important work for the leader." After all, as management thinker Warren Bennis has observed, "None of us is as smart as all of us." Yet Tunnicliffe says that honesty requires him to admit that "I spent a long time talking about enabling, but really providing, solutions. . . . I have finally concluded that my role must change from doing the task to enabling. Doing the task is an indulgence. The leader needs to recognize [that] he can't do it all by himself."

Describing what he calls his "turning point," Tunnicliffe remembers:

London Underground was facing a potential strike by the drivers. With nearly one million travelers dependent on the Underground each day, this has a profound effect on transportation into and around the city, and the ability of a large part of the working population to get to work.

I briefed the Industrial Relations team on this occasion. The team understood the seriousness of the situation. My brief to them was, "Take the moral high ground. Don't piss off the drivers. They are strategic. Do your best." They said, "What should we do first?" I said, "I don't know." I paced around a little and left the room.

When I got home, my wife, Sue, said, "The strike is over. I saw it on television."

I felt very good, and I had not given them the answer. I also felt good because my actions had been consistent with a key principle I had been articulating, but not always behaving consistently with. It was particularly satisfying because of the scale and consequences of the problem. It made teamwork for everyone easier from that point on.

Create self-confidence.

If middle managers and frontline workers are going to change their behavior and develop new skills, they must have—or acquire—self-confidence. Only then can they begin to use authority more effectively in their area of responsibility.

Bernard Fournier of Rank Xerox makes the point:

> The single most important factor in achieving breakthrough with middle managers is creating confidence. Empowerment is not a problem for a manager who is strong and confident. A successful manager is one who will risk failure to achieve success. The key to the middle management problem is to provide [managers] with the confidence to take risks and the capability to complete the task.

Jan Carlzon reinforced and developed this theme. Here is what he told me:

> You create self-confidence. People aren't born with self-confidence. It comes through success and experience and the environment. . . .
>
> The most important role of the leader is to create confidence among people. They must dare to take risks and responsibility. The worst thing is that people are afraid of their jobs and lack of confidence. The solution is a lot of education and communication. The leader must live up to what he says. And you must back them up if they make mistakes, not punish them. My principal role is to widen, and create confidence. A leader can do the reverse. He can create a loss of confidence.
>
> An important question for every leader is how to build a management system related to the responsibility and the authority you give away. If you tell an individual, "I want you to give good service but I will measure you on your budget," it doesn't work. Asking people to provide good service but not providing the resources just doesn't work. Service means more than having a product . . . service is quick response and being on time.

Our business is not to sell a ticket at SAS, but to get customers back for a second, third, or fourth time. We get there by the way we serve our customers. Having said this, my role is to create confidence.

Then Carlzon took out a piece of paper and drew a figure.

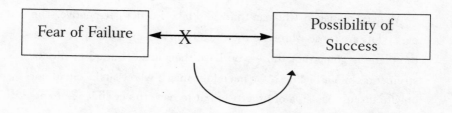

"My role is to create confidence"

"How far are you prepared to go toward failure?" he asked. He made a mark between the point in the center of the diagram and the box on the left labeled "Fear of failure." He then marked the same distance between the center and the box on the right labeled "Possibility of success." I suggest that leaders perform this exercise too.

"The difference," he said, "between this point and success is the efficiency of management. The single most important factor in achieving breakthrough with middle management is creating confidence with these individuals. Once this is achieved, they can address the skill and behavior issues."

Gene Fife had an insightful way of addressing the same subject.

We ask everyone in Goldman Sachs, "What is your unique source of competitive advantage?" People need to think in these terms. They need to connect their unique individual qualities with their contribution to achieving the team's and then the organization's objectives.

"Why do you get the business?" is the most important question for our business developers. People having confidence in themselves and understanding their unique source of competitive advantage is a precondition for taking on responsibility. We give people responsibility early in Goldman Sachs. You don't have to be 40 years old to do something. Both young analysts and vice presidents go in front of the client.

We need managers who can think and take a wider perspective. The best pilots are those who have their heads up and are looking at where the plane is going, not those who have their heads buried in the instruments. In our business, we need [a manager who visits] a client not only to discuss his area of expertise, but to have the confidence to explore other opportunities where our financial services might apply.

Recently, a [securities] expert came back and the company he was dealing with was about to sell a particular division. "We might be able to help," he said. Had he stuck to his narrow role and not had the confidence to explore other areas, we never would have heard of that business. We need that entrepreneurial instinct, not a bland risk-averse approach which bores the pants off the client.

A Unilever team had the following experience relevant to the subject of collective self-confidence. After the team described future and emerging customer needs, a senior executive disagreed—and did so using his very best authoritative tone—which in the past would have silenced junior workers. A young manager confronted him directly and explained how his assumptions and opinions were flawed. The group had done their work and stood by it. Examples of this happened over and over. No one could have confronted the CEO alone. Collective self-confidence enabled a new strategy to be developed—bottom up.

Distinguish between internal operational problems and external strategic problems, both of which may involve technical and adaptive work.

When you hand over a problem, be aware of the two basic categories of problems and adjust your expectations accordingly.

Technical solutions are clearly visible and understood, and the skills to carry them out are readily available. As I said earlier, the key to solving technical problems lies in properly executing strategy. Adaptive work, on the other hand, requires people to learn the new and unlearn the old. The solution is unclear. No one has the exact answer. Because new logic is involved, people must examine deeply held beliefs and assumptions about their work and their company.

Andrew Parkinson, president and chief executive officer of Peapod, Inc., an online grocery company with headquarters in Skokie, Illinois, relates the difficulty he had in shedding old ways to deal with problems in the vastly different world of Internet grocery sales. Formerly with Procter & Gamble, Parkinson said he had to unlearn "everything I knew about anything," dispensing with the managerial habits of a lifetime: "During my years at Procter & Gamble, I learned a logical, process-oriented, methodical way of introducing and marketing new products. We were indoctrinated in the four Ps . . . product, packaging, price, promotion—and in product testing to the nth degree within a very hierarchical structure."

As he would soon discover, however, the P&G approach of testing in small markets and expanding slowly had about as much relevance to cyberspace as buttonhooks have to high-top sneakers. The brick-and-mortar ways of bringing products to market, managing people, and making decisions simply did not work in the Internet world.

Who cares about packaging, for instance? The on-screen information about products is far more important, Parkinson was forced to admit. "And as we adjusted to the Web's demands for quicker decisionmaking and quicker implementation, we found ourselves failing a lot."

What kind of (mostly adaptive) solution has Parkinson implemented? "I've had to learn to become comfortable with a continual-improvement approach to doing business," he answered, leaving behind the "perfect up-front approach" learned at P&G. That's a good thing because the model will "always be evolving."For instance, Parkinson now knows that the picking, packing, and grocery delivery processes that are working for him today in one centralized distribution center, doing $30 million worth of business, will have to be revamped as the business grows. Constant evolution is the name of the game in today's world—a difficult lesson Parkinson hopes he has mastered.

Remember that people must commit to one another before they will commit to a strategy.

It is important to monitor the commitment of your workers to their fellow employees, since that commitment is a precondition for their allegiance to your strategy. If you hand over a problem, make sure that the people who receive it mutually trust and respect each other. That trust must precede effective collective action toward the common goal.

In a recent speech, Walter V. Shipley, former chairman and chief executive officer of Chase Manhattan Corporation, recalled asking Bill Russell, legendary star of the Boston Celtics, what made his championship team tick. Russell replied that it was the trust each player had in his teammates, in their abilities, and in the coach's direction. Or, as a successful college football coach once put it, "We play with one heartbeat."

Feedback is crucial for keeping track of how people are relating to one another. "Teams are everything at Goldman Sachs," Gene Fife told me. "So it's vital that the individual also understands the perspective of colleagues who work with him or her day in and day out." To promote that understanding, Goldman uses a peer appraisal system that lets each senior executive know how he or she is perceived by colleagues.

The idea of teamwork does not come easily to some organizations, and Jan Timmer of Philips places the blame squarely on the leader's shoulders. "We need to learn to work in teams, [and there is] an emerging class of young people that comes easily to the idea of working together toward a common goal. They think less about power and position. These young people want to be actively involved. It's the boss that holds them back." Younger people cross boundaries—functional, geographic, business, and so forth—more easily. According to Timmer, "We need to learn to give them more space."

Larry Bossidy would no doubt agree with Timmer's assessment, but he once explained the underlying problem this way: "Most older executives earned their stripes by completing assigned tasks competently. The hierarchical organization of American corporations fostered a system that allowed talented lone rangers to rise through the ranks." Despite comments about how lonely it was at the top or in their isolated corner offices, many executives liked it that way, Bossidy noted, because the system made it possible for them to stand out by dint of brains and hard work.

It should come as no surprise, then, that some leaders are drawn to subordinates who emulate this behavior—even though, as Bossidy states emphatically, this type of organization is obsolete. In fact, he flatly rejects such lone-ranger behavior as destructive to the organization and something that can no longer be rewarded, "no matter how impressive the achievements." Leadership that "includes communication, teamwork, and an obsession with satisfying customers" is the kind of behavior that earns rewards at AlliedSignal these days.

At Johnson & Johnson, Ralph Larsen describes "creating a bias for action" as a focus on growth, and helping people to achieve this ambition by providing them with opportunities to grow and the funds with which to do it. After my talk with

Larsen, I am convinced that when J&J managers come to the executive committee with a project, they get the sense that the company is not interested in tearing a proposal apart or finding fault with its presentation. Instead they are made to feel what Larsen already knows: "We are looking for ways to make it better . . . to make sure the deal gets done. . . . It really becomes much more of a conversation and a collaborative effort." If Timmer, Bossidy, and Larsen are right, and I think that they are, we will not be able to help employees assume more responsibility until we transform the conventional thinking at the organization's top.

Look upon diverse points of view as valuable, not problematic.

People's diverse backgrounds and experiences are invaluable because we learn from them. When a leader assigns a problem, try to make sure that a diverse team will review the new plans and tackle the proposal. Then, as John Nordstrom advises, "Listen, listen, listen." Realize that the varying perspectives of other executives emerge from different experiences and perceptions, and "understanding them as best you can and trusting them is very important."

Also, encourage open discussion. "I've learned the hard way that a person who has unresolved questions may just be right," Ralph Larsen told me. "I want to try to understand where he or she is coming from. Once I understand, I might disagree and say, 'We're not going to do it that way,' but at least the unspoken issue is on the table."

John Nordstrom goes even further, perhaps because his is a family-owned firm in which all top managers have risen through the ranks. Nordstrom points out that "these people know what they are doing," he says, "even if they seem to be [doing] crazy things. When we see resistance . . . we let them get on with it and later discover they were usually right."

Allow people to take risks and support them when they make mistakes.

Jan Carlzon believes that people must be encouraged to dare, to take risks, and to assume responsibility. He also thinks that the leader must back them up even when they make mistakes since, at some point, we all do.

When you hand over a problem, make sure the recipients understand that you want their best response—even if it contradicts existing policy and involves greater risk than usual. If the company penalizes risk taking and rewards performing by rote, people will continue avoiding responsibility and will perform at a level that is less than their best. If, throughout the organization a process which examines who makes decisions and how they do so is under way, it is of primary importance that all involved are offered opportunities to further develop their skills and knowledge. The leader needs, also, to encourage curiosity about the problem-solving process, and spur independent thinking and action in frontline workers.

Here is what Ralph Larsen told me about the importance of providing support to managers:

The one thing I've learned more than anything else in this job is that if you really make it hard for people, you can wear this organization out to the point where you will slow the organization in extraordinary ways. Opportunities will not come to you, will not ever rise to the level of the executive committee. If somebody knows they're going to come in and get beaten up and interrogated and made a fool of or put on the spot, they are going to be less apt to bring you the opportunity.

Having said that, if you create a different kind of environment which says we know you're smart, know you're well-intentioned, know your objectives are the same as ours, you want to grow this business , . . . we may not think this is the greatest deal in the world and will ask a lot of questions, and make sure that it's consistent with our long-term strategy. But at the end of the day, we have an enormous amount of respect for you as an individual for what you're trying to accomplish, and we want to help. That's the tone that I have tried to set.

People need to feel that a safety net is in place before they go too far out on a limb. They must be allowed to make mistakes, learn from them, and go on to perform their "personal best" for their organizations. After all, no progress is made without mistakes.

As Leslie H. Wexner, founder, chairman, and chief executive officer of The Limited, Inc., states: "I want our people to hit home runs, but remember that when Babe Ruth was the home run king, he also led the league in strikeouts."

Having said that, I am not implying that people can go about willy-nilly making bad decisions indefinitely without fear of consequence. It is up to the leader to stop the cycle when responsibility is being poorly handled, just as the leader must make it clear that those who refuse to assume responsibility are jeopardizing their careers. The leader obviously walks a fine line between being supportive and maintaining order.

Select the right people.

A leader may try to engender confidence, offer independence, and support risk taking by employees, yet find it difficult to break the stranglehold of a traditional, conservative perspective. The remnants of the old hierarchical, command-and-control, risk-averse environment continues to pervade too many organizations. Responsibility was never encouraged, thus none was taken.

In that event, a blood transfusion may be the only solution. To foster responsibility in all corners of the organization, Gene Fife of Goldman Sachs minces no words: "Clear out the dead wood. Hire people you consider better than yourself. Train them and give them feedback. Make sure your code of ethics and values are core in your appraisal and promotion process." On the same subject, Norman Sanson of McKinsey told me: "We need to hire people who can lead without the authority to lead. People fail because we hire wrong. To make matters worse, one weak person will make four project teams 28 percent less effective."

Therefore, counterbalance the deadly burden of hardened perceptions and opinions with enthusiastic newcomers. Their openness to change and their willingness to become caught up in the excitement of stretching ambition can incite a healthier attitude toward increased responsibility throughout the organization. Remember, your credibility is at stake. Take action sooner rather than later.

Next

In the final chapter, I offer some of the questions that leaders ask me about their work—and my answers.

11

Questions and Answers

THE BUSINESS OF BUSINESS IS GROWTH. Survival in today's economy depends on it. Since customers underwrite growth, I might be accurate to say: "The business of business is customers." That is where value resides—not in the product or service, but in the customer.

Part of the real work of leaders, then, is to make their organizations more attuned to customers' whims and more adept at meeting their needs. Developing new customers and surpassing competitors in the fight to retain them, however, is getting tougher by the minute. And leaders know it. Given the prevailing climate, it is no surprise that the leaders I work with frequently look for advice on how to make their organizations more responsive to customers. Many of the questions they ask me are directly related to the customer; all are aimed at making their organizations work in ways that will ultimately serve the customer. Here is a sample of the kinds of questions they ask:

In an age when focusing on the customer seems to be the business mantra, why is it that relatively few of us get great marks in this area?

I suspect it relates to companies' inability to truly inject the customer and customer data into the heart of the organization. Sure, leaders talk a good game and spend millions of dollars trying to understand customers and markets, but the customers' priorities are not really management's priorities. That is, internal financial guidelines, not the customer, still drive the resource allocation process.

Customer research usually gives a pretty clear picture of what determines purchase decisions and indicates why customers migrate to competitors. More often than not, however, management treats this information as "interesting" instead of "crucial," and does not use it to make critical decisions about administrative infrastructure. Take the telecommunications industry, for example. Customer data points to different levels of service requirements—some customers need service in thirty seconds, others in thirty minutes, and others in twenty-four hours. Typically, telecom companies' service response times falls somewhere between one to eight hours and is unspecified, thereby addressing few, if any, of the individual customer's requirements. In addition, the internal measures imposed on the service engineer are more likely to include controls over the use of spare parts rather than checks on whether service is available when customers need it.

Customers tell me how important an employee's attitude is. Yet I have never met a vice president in charge of friendliness or a director of responsiveness. Salespeople and administrative people are rated and rewarded according to tough internal standards that do not even vaguely resemble customer concerns. Billing departments, for example, pay attention to how much time is outstanding on payments, but never look at the reasons for the delays. Customers feel company staffs are trained to "tighten the noose with friendliness," as opposed to being genuinely helpful in solving a short-term problem.

What does all this mean to the long-term health of companies? Precisely this: Leaders who are serious about the imperative to focus the company on growth need to pay more than lip service to the people who facilitate that process. It is time to repair the estrangement between how customers offer feedback and how resources are allocated within the organization.

Sir Peter Bonfield, former chairman at British information technology provider ICL and currently the chief executive officer of British Telecom, was blunt when he told me: "If you are serious about customer responsiveness, pay people for customer responsiveness." Recalling the method used at ICL, Bonfield said that "15 percent of the manager's bonus was measured on customer service; 20 percent on the profit and loss of the business. We did an outside survey to measure improvement from a defined base of customer satisfaction, which is specifically designed for each business. If customer satisfaction didn't improve, the manager got zippo for this portion of the bonus."

How do we find the right tools or standards for measuring a company's performance in the area of responding to customers, and then get those tools aligned in support of long-term performance?

That's a tough question, because many familiar measures and standards emphasize control more than adaptive change. There is a great deal of uncertainty both about how and what to measure in a changing environment. As Denis Tunnicliffe of London Underground rightly points out, the fact that "we don't measure something . . . doesn't mean it doesn't exist." Denis is convinced that "we measure irrelevant things because they are easy to measure, and don't measure many critical things because they are intangible or difficult to measure."

Denis observes that in the workplace, for example, management knows it has to create a good employee environment. So it measures itself in terms of pay and benefits, and finds that it is performing well. Nevertheless, employees still are unhappy working there. Obviously, "unhappiness" should be measured, but management doesn't know how. The bottom line is, according to Denis, "it's not the sum of the parts," Tunnicliffe says, but that "doesn't mean it's not an important point of every manager's job."

And he's right, of course.

So is Syd Pennington, managing director of Virgin Atlantic Airways Ltd., when he says that "London [stock exchange] is obsessed with short-term gains; that's what really drives measures." Syd adds that his boss, Richard Branson, founder and chairman of the Virgin Group, measures success differently. "He gets a big kick out of [Virgin] being airline of the year, publishing letters from satisfied customers. . . . These are more important to him than the bottom line. We believe that will secure the bottom line."

Branson's philosophy is supported by Alfie Kohn, a well-known writer and lecturer on human behavior, who contends that "when you do something for a reward, you tend to become less interested in what you're doing. It becomes something of a chore, something you have to get through in order to pick up the dollar or the 'A' or an extra dessert."

The core of Kohn's thinking—and its most controversial aspect—is his insistence that not only do material rewards not motivate well, but they actually poison natural motivators such as curiosity and self-esteem.

Obviously, companies are not going to do away with rewards. Although employees' personal satisfaction may be critical to their performance, people still need to earn money. What businesses can and must do, however, is reverse the "mental set" of organizations, starting with their leaders. Here is what I mean. Most organizations start with strategy and objectives and build management systems, organizational structures, and business processes based on internal standards. Companies have to flip the process to start with customer priorities; they motivate each aspect of the infrastructure—standards, measures, rewards, processes, delivery, and management systems. Once the customer becomes the primary consideration in making decisions, the company has the opportunity to align all the elements.

On a practical level, can leaders teach employees to be attuned to customers' needs?

Not entirely. You can polish behavior and target specific activities or processes for improvement. If you haven't hired the right people in the first place, all is for naught—particularly in this area. Jan Timmer of Philips Electronics says customer responsiveness is a state of mind. He juxtaposes the sad tale of the now-extinct Eastern Airlines against the success enjoyed by Delta Air Lines to make his point:

With their lack of respect for customers, Eastern Airlines never had a chance. They treated customers like cattle. The staff felt that was the way in which they were treated, of course, but it didn't matter. Every flier I know would avoid Eastern like the plague.

Delta, on the other hand, came out of a Southern tradition where respect is a centerpiece of society. Delta recruited from its population of friendly, conscientious, and respectful people. It made a marked difference in how customers were treated as people. I would try to see if Delta had a flight to my next destination for the same reason I would avoid Eastern—the people they hired.

Timmer's experience reminded me of a story Tom Peters once told me about the Connecticut grocer, Stu Leonard. After spending a day in the store, Tom asked Stu how he trained people to be so nice. "We don't train people to be nice," replied Stu. "We hire nice people; we train people to use our cash registers."

Can you suggest a process for young, relatively inexperienced leaders who are intent on making customers their highest priority?

Determine what drives you toward and away from the customer. The leader's frame of mind and, by extension, that of the whole organization, must believe in the following: Let the customer define the requirement and the need; let the front line identify the "inhibitors" (the factors preventing or stalling their attempts to fulfill the requirement); let management support the front line by removing the inhibitors. This requires management to listen to customers and to the front line to determine what processes need to be continued or stopped.

First, meet with a group of frontline people from varied departments within the company—sales, service, administration, and so forth, and a similar group from research and development, manufacturing, and distribution. Ask them what they believe management wants them to achieve. Listen very closely. See if their views reflect the company's vision or ambition. If not, rethink the ambition. Is it credible? Is it clear and simple? Can the average working person in the organization understand and relate to it?

Next, consider which of the multiple projects the company is currently pursuing will help to achieve the ambition. Decide what can be abandoned for now, so that more time and energy can be devoted to top priorities. Try creating a "let's stop doing a few things" suggestion box. Ask people for feedback, remain open-minded, and do not protect sacred cows. For example, resist the temptation to justify the need for large numbers of financial controllers; do not feel compelled to hold onto every bit of information that the leader and teams have requested from the field. Develop a formula for calculating the cost of each activity, process, or initiative. Use the criteria of payback to customers. If it doesn't yield a payback, stop doing it. If the customer isn't willing to pay for it, why should the company?

An interesting way to gauge customer payback is to imagine taking a customer through several headquarters-driven initiatives. Ask the customer which ones he or she is willing to pay for. Then, imagine consulting with the customer regarding which initiatives make sense and will improve the company's capacity to deliver value-added products and services. Through the customer's eyes, review the computerized billing system, financial controls, management systems, and so forth. Lay out the costs of each process in human and capital terms. Does the customer think it's worth it?

The point here is to recognize that it is the customer who pays your salary. Assume that he or she is willing to underwrite only activities that improve the ability to meet customers' requirements and to remove frontline inhibitors. Vow to stop projects that fall into neither category. Be ruthless! The future of the organization is at stake.

The entire top team must share this all-encompassing focus on the customer. Consider team members and ask yourself: Does the team contain the right skills? Are the members' management styles consistent with the culture I am trying to create? Are they team players? Figure out how to improve the quality of teamwork throughout the organization, starting with the leader and the team. Finally, hold steady and be brave. Many people fear change; a significant facet of the leader's role, to make the company more responsive to customers, is that of change agent. If naysayers are allowed to kill your idea, the leader will die with it—because there will be nothing left to lead.

How can a leader make sure he or she has the "right" top team?

First of all, having a committed team is a precondition for success. Therefore, do not venture far into any problem-solving initiative without the top team's pledge of agreement to the vision, strategy, and objectives of the business. Think about the abilities the management team requires. Assess whether individuals are ready for change and their capacity to work together to realize an ambition.

Specifically, ask what individual strengths and weaknesses exist. What drives and motivates each person?

Recognize and acknowledge behavior that may impede the project. Offer and receive feedback regarding how effectively an individual works with the top team. Establish a six-month formal review as well as informal procedures when required. Spend a lot of time on the subject of the team's composition and do not hesitate to replace executives who oppose your initiative and are unable or unwilling to change. They are likely to sabotage team decisions.

When screening new applicants, the most important criterion is teamwork. I am reminded of a Stanford University engineer who returned from interviewing at Hewlett-Packard, where he was surprised that no one asked about his engineering skill or achievements. The entire focus was on his ability to work on a team. An HP executive explained the rationale: The interviewers assumed he had the necessary engineering skills; if not, he would not have passed the initial screening and gotten to the interview process. According to the HP executive, if the young man joined Hewlett-Packard, he would spend "the next twenty-five years working in teams. If he can't work in teams, he will be unable to apply his engineering skills." HP enjoys the luxury of being an "employer of choice." According to Chairman Lew Platt, "If you go to the business schools, or the graduate schools of engineering, or even the undergraduate schools of engineering, you will find that in most surveys HP finishes first or very close to the top. That gives us access to great people. We have a turnover rate which is somewhere between a third and a fourth our industry average . . . [offering us a] tremendous competitive advantage. Imagine the energy we don't spend recruiting and bringing new people on board."

Create intimacy and trust with your team by spending as much time as possible helping people understand the difficult issues that are evoked by change. Get to know team members personally. That means setting aside unstructured time at the office, as well as outside time for socializing with each individual and the group.

Leaders managing adaptive-change agendas must be ruthlessly honest with themselves regarding the commitment, or lack of it, from individual team members both to one another and to the leader's ambition. Liam Strong, chief executive officer of British retailer Sears plc, reminded me that "the great enemy is pride in the past." Frequently, people would like to change, but are unable to do so. The credibility of the leader is affected directly by his or her ability to build an effective team, and, as Strong pointed out, time is critical.

The leader depends on the workforce to deliver improved business performance, financial results, renewal, and adaptive change. Employees know full well whether the top team is effective and will respond accordingly.

How can a leader facilitate the learning and unlearning that has to precede adaptive change?

The key is to put oneself in other people's shoes. Think about how the typical employee approaches his or her job. Everyone goes to work ready to do their jobs within the context of internal ground rules and certain expectations of behavior and performance. These rules and expectations have developed over time to the point where everyone considers him- or herself an expert in the job. If employees thought there was a better way to do the job, they probably would have started operating that way already. The leader has to take the time to help them unlearn what they think is the right way so their minds and hearts are able to consider the new way.

Unlearning begins when the leader and the top team set a context wherein people gain new insights into the leader's ideas, which in turn motivates them to think and work in a new way. The body of the organization is much more likely to draw conclusions similar to those of top management if they feel they have been on a journey with the leader, during which the leader details his or her ambition and shows where the organization has been and where it hopes to go. Hopefully, the leader can point out how this path differs from those traveled in the past and specifies what the new direction means for each person in his or her area of responsibility. Thus, the leader makes explicit what the organization needs to learn and how people can begin the process of learning it. As Bernard Fournier of Rank Xerox puts it, "We have to learn how to learn."

Too often, though, executives devote large amounts of time to devise the strategy, but not enough time to determine precisely what knowledge is required to implement it effectively. They compound the problem by moving too quickly toward directing an audience that frequently has its own perceptions and opinions regarding what should be done and why. Of course, it is best to get off to a good start in communicating, so that subsequent communication is not fragmented, further obscuring the implementation process.

What should a leader do to prevent stress and distress at a company that is in the midst of adaptive change?

Do not even try. It's important to accept that a certain level of distress is actually a prerequisite to change. It may feel counterintuitive, but one critical aspect of the leader's work is to maintain, not stifle, a level of disequilibrium that will push people to work on solving the stress-producing problems. In essence, leaders preempt psychological mechanisms that allow employees to avoid the hard and necessary work required to manage change. At the same time, leaders create conditions within which groups throughout the organization can accept responsibility for finding solutions.

That means going against the grain. Rather than fulfilling workers' expectations for answers, the leader provides only questions; instead of quelling conflict, the leader generates it; instead of maintaining norms, he or she challenges them; rather than orienting people to their current roles, the leader disorients them so that new roles and new relationships can develop. In short, the leader resists the urge to protect and, instead, allows people to experience an outside threat to unite them in an effort to conquer the threatening force. Helping people implement adaptive change is the difference between genuine leadership and mere authority.

Of course, real life is fluid, so a leader will have to adjust his or her response depending on the severity of the problem, the resilience of the organization, and the ripeness of the issue. Distress must not be allowed to build to the point where people are immobilized.

How can you nurture leaders at all levels of an organization?

By mobilizing people to engage in their work and giving them the opportunities to define, refine, and solve their own problems. Too often, leaders rush in to save the day when a threat arises. Not surprisingly, employees, who face complex and frustrating challenges in their jobs daily, want support and guidance. They also press for answers to problems that seem complex and possibly intractable. They hanker for a structure that offers order and security.

When leaders give in to employees' unrealistic demands or wishes for a savior, they are actually denying the employees an important opportunity to develop their own problem-solving skills. They are denying them the chance to acquire leadership characteristics. By distributing authority to make decisions throughout the organization, leaders encourage a process that will enable the next generation of leaders to come of age with a sophisticated understanding in the concept of adaptive work. Remember, the leader's role is not to do all the work, but rather to frame the challenges and create the conditions that will enable the business to grow with speed.

Epilogue:
The Value
Leaders Add

OFTEN ASK SENIOR MANAGERS what people should thank them for today (meaning the work they've done in recent years) and five years from now. I frame this question by reminding members of the top team that they have to clarify that very issue for others.

Specifically, I say, "If I invited a salesperson or an assembly-line worker to meet with you and your executive team next Tuesday and gave him or her twenty or thirty minutes to say 'thank you,' what would the person thank you for?" Some leaders are a little embarrassed and silenced by this question; others can articulate an answer clearly and immediately.

Executives of IBM U.K., for example, said "not much" after their company was held responsible for one-fifth of the parent company's $5 billion loss. That response was mirrored by managers one and two levels down, which is not uncommon in situations where leadership is underperforming.

Ralph Larsen, on the other hand, states clearly that people within J&J should thank us for focusing our eyes on growth, creating a bias for action, and creating an environment where we can do important work in health care. And his people concur.

It is part of the real work of a leader to provide direction and to create the conditions for people throughout the organization to become the best they can be, able to move into their futures rather than stuck in the past.

The thank-you question is another way of asking, what is the collective value added of the leader and the executive team. I believe that what I am referring to as value added is the team's capacity for collective action on issues requiring cabinet-level responsibility, just as much as it is the team's ability to make what Gene Fife of Goldman Sachs calls a "special place" where people want to come to work, contribute, and achieve.

You probably recall Leo Tolstoy's opening words in *Anna Karenina*: "All happy families resemble one another. Every unhappy family is unhappy in its own way." Companies are like that. Faltering companies produce their own peculiar versions of corporate misery, but the successes are amazingly similar. Companies that function brilliantly in a kaleidoscopic era—the ones that keep adapting and growing without losing their way—tend to have certain traits in common.

Companies that achieve their ambition are nearly always run by people who value leadership over authority. By authority, I mean the blatant power to order individuals to perform in specific ways. Authority generally produces limited results. Leadership, on the other hand, is the far more challenging and sophisticated ability to inspire a staff of diverse workers to do great things together, notably to focus their collective intelligence on the company's adaptive work.

Performing the act of leadership, which is difficult at any level of an organization, involves, but is not limited to, the following: the demands to create a stretching ambition and deliver the annual plan; increase productivity and innovation at the same time; engage people in the work that only they can do, while accelerating the pace of change to a level many feel is too fast; es-

tablish values that guide behavior while recognizing the countervalues. These responsibilities present every leader with para-
doxes. It is exhaustive work.

Hold steady, maintain the focus of your ambition, frame the
next leadership challenge, and use your people as valued resources as you collectively solve problems and learn your way
into the future. Be decisive and discover the power of questions.

Sources

THIS BOOK IS BASED ON my observations as an adviser to *Fortune* 1000 companies and on more than forty interviews I conducted with senior executives.

Other sources include:

Preface

James Champy, *Reengineering Management* (New York: HarperBusiness, 1995).

Ram Charan and Geoffrey Colvin, "Why CEOs Fail," *Fortune*, June 21, 1999.

Ronald A. Heifetz, *Leadership Without Easy Answers* (Cambridge, Mass.: Harvard University Press, 1994).

"Hot Seat in the Corner Office," *Business Week*, February 14, 2000.

Chapter 1

Lawrence A. Bossidy, speech, Economic Club of Washington, Washington, D.C., June 19, 1996.

Ram Charan and Geoffrey Colvin, "Why CEOs Fail," *Fortune*, June 21, 1999.

James Champy and Nitin Nohria, *The Arc of Ambition* (Cambridge, Mass.: Perseus Books, 2000).

Michael Fradette and Steve Michaud, *Corporate Kinetics* (New York: Simon & Schuster, 1998).

Daniel McGinn with Rich Thomas, "A Star Image Blurs," *Newsweek*, April 6, 1998.

Eloise Salholz, "Noriega's Surrender," *Newsweek*, January 15, 1990.

Geoffrey Smith, "Film Versus Digital," *Business Week*, August 2, 1999.

Joseph B. Treaster, "The 1992 Campaign," *New York Times,* July 28, 1992.

"Bush Requests $5.9 Billion in FY 1990," *Alcoholism & Drug Abuse Week,* February 15, 1989.

"Carp Set to Succeed Fisher as Kodak CEO," *Chain Drug Review*, June 28, 1999. URL: www.state.ak.us/local/akpages/FISH.GAME/notebook/biggame/muskoxen.htm.

Chapter 2

Donald L. Boudreau, speech, "American Banker's Best Practices in Retail Banking Symposium," February 25, 1998.

Jan Carlzon, *Moments of Truth* (New York: Harper & Row, 1987).

Polly LaBarre, "Leaders.com," *Fast Company*, June 1999.

Ralph S. Larsen, "FrameworkS—Turning the Challenges of Change into Opportunities for Growth," *Chief Executive*, May 1, 1999.

"Virtuoso Who Rates Success by Bright Eyes," *Financial Times*, November 3, 1998.

Chapter 3

James Champy, *Reengineering Management* (New York: HarperBusiness, 1995).

Ralph S. Larsen, "FrameworkS—Turning the Challenges of Change into Opportunities for Growth," *Chief Executive*, May 1, 1999.

Anna Muoio, "The Art of Smart," *Fast Company*, July-August 1999.

Chapter 4

Lawrence A. Bossidy, speech, Economic Club of Washington, Washington, D.C., June 19, 1996.

James Champy, *Reengineering Management* (New York: HarperBusiness, 1995).

Jan Carlzon, *Moments of Truth* (New York: Harper & Row, 1987).

Ralph S. Larsen, "FrameworkS—Turning the Challenges of Change into Opportunities for Growth," *Chief Executive*, May 1, 1999.

George A. Loch, speech, "Transforming a Corporate Culture to Master Change," CEO Series, July 1996.

Anna Muoio, "The Art of Smart," *Fast Company*, July-August 1999.

Laura Pedersen, "Earning it—Minding Your Business," *New York Times*, September 10, 1995.

Evan Ramstad and Jon G. Auerbach, "Behind Digital's Downfall," *Wall Street Journal*, January 28, 1998.

Steven Pearlstein, "Reinventing Xerox Corporation," *Washington Post*, June 29, 1998.

William C. Taylor, "The Leader of the Future," *Fast Company*, June 1999.

John F. Welch, Jr., "Speed, Simplicity, Self-Confidence—An Interview with Jack Welch, *Harvard Business Review*, September-October 1989.

www.xerox.com.

Chapter 5

Lawrence A. Bossidy, speech, Economic Club of Washington, Washington, D.C., June 19, 1996.

Jan Carlzon, *Moments of Truth* (New York: Harper & Row, 1987).

Thomas L. Friedman, *The Lexus and the Olive Tree* (New York: Farrar, Straus and Girous, 1999).

Alan Goldstein, "When the Chips Are Down," *Dallas Morning News*, February 3, 1996.

John Jesitus, "Engineered for Success," *Industry Week,* July 19, 1999.

Kavita Kaur, "Apple iMac," *Computers Today*, July 31, 1999.

Michael Krantz, "Steve's Two Jobs," *Time*, October 18, 1999.

John F. Welch, Lawrence Bossidy, William Weiss, Michael Walsh, and Stratford Sherman, "A Master Class in Radical Change," *Fortune*, December 13, 1993.

Chapter 6

Charles Fishman, "Whole Foods Is All Teams," *Fast Company*, April 1996.

Michael Fradette and Steve Michaud, *Corporate Kinetics* (New York: Simon & Schuster, 1998).

Chapter 7

Michael Fradette and Steve Michaud, *Corporate Kinetics* (New York: Simon & Schuster, 1998).

Chapter 8

Jay A. Conger, Gretchen M. Spreitzer, and Edward E. Lawler III, *The Change Leaders Handbook* (San Francisco: Jossey-Bass, Inc., 1999).

Anna Muoio, "The Art of Smart," *Fast Company*, July-August 1999.

Chapter 9

Ronald A. Heifetz, *Leadership Without Easy Answers* (Cambridge, Mass.: Harvard University Press, 1994).

Andrew S. Grove, *Only the Paranoid Survive* (New York: Bantam Doubleday Dell, 1996).

Nina Munk, "How Levi's Trashed a Great American Brand," *Fortune*, April 12, 1999.

William C. Taylor, "The Leader of the Future," *Fast Company*, June 1999.

Chapter 10

Jan Carlzon, *Moments of Truth* (New York: Harper & Row, 1987).

Jay A. Conger, Gretchen M. Spreitzer, and Edward E. Lawler III, *The Change Leaders Handbook* (San Francisco: Jossey-Bass, Inc., 1999).

Anna Muoio, "The Art of Smart," *Fast Company*, July-August 1999.

Leslie H. Wexner, "Letter to Shareholders," The Limited, Inc., 1998 *Annual Report*.

Index